"An easy-to-use and practical handbook for anyone seeking to live life fully. Douglas Bloch skillfully and with great insight guides the reader to the most important discovery anyone can make—the discovery of the inner voice."
Mary and Haven Boggs, directors of
Living Enrichment Center

"Douglas Bloch's affirmations are healing and empowering, helping the reader to remember and renew the all-important connection to spirit, the very source of guidance and love."
Joan Borysenko, author of *Minding*
the Body, Mending the Mind

"Spiritual 'bites' to stimulate a richer perspective and bring renewal to all who need it."
Marilyn Ferguson, author of
The Aquarian Conspiracy

"Thank you for your beautiful, inspiring writing. *Listening to Your Inner Voice* will help to guide many thousands of people into greater freedom, joy, peace, and wholeness through the truth that it teaches and exemplifies."
Kathy Juline, editor,
Science of Mind magazine

"*Listening to Your Inner Voice* provides the reader with empowering and practical messages that can be used to add focus and provide comfort to us all."
Rokelle Lerner, author of *Daily*
Affirmations for Adult Children of
Alcoholics and *Affirmations for the*
Inner Child

"A wonderful guide to promoting high self-value and inner confidence through the affirmation process."
Dennis Wholey, author of
The Courage to Change and
Becoming Your Own Parent

Listening To Your Inner Voice

Discover the Truth Within You and Let It Guide Your Way

Douglas Bloch

CompCare® Publishers
2415 Annapolis Lane, Minneapolis, MN 55441

Library of Congress Cataloging-in-Publication Data
Bloch, Douglas, 1949-
    Listening to your inner voice : discover the truth within
you and let it direct your way / Douglas Bloch.
        p.   cm.
    ISBN 0-89638-253-2
    1. Spiritual life.   2. Meditations.   I. Title.
BL624-B43   1991
241.4--dc20   91-23780
                                                        CIP

Cover design by Lois Stanfield
The quotation on page 1 is excerpted from *Living in the Light* by
Shakti Gawain. Copyright 1986 by Shakti Gawain. Reprinted
by permission of New World Library, San Rafael, California.

Inquiries, orders, and catalog requests should be addressed to:
CompCare Publishers
2415 Annapolis Lane
Minneapolis, Minnesota 55441
612/559-4800 or toll free 800/328-3330

6   5   4   3   2
96 95 94 93 92 91

And I have the firm belief in this now, not only in terms of my own experience but in knowing about the experience of others, that when you follow your bliss, doors will open where you would not have thought there were going to be doors and where there wouldn't be a door for anybody else.

Joseph Campbell

for Joan

CONTENTS

Listening to your inner voice means . . .
    . . . to go within and find your sense of purpose.

CONTENTS

CONTENTS

CONTENTS

. . . to reap the rewards of a joyful and peaceful life.

ACKNOWLEDGMENTS

Many individuals have inspired me to get in touch with and trust my inner voice. To begin, I once again acknowledge Eileen Caddy and the Findhorn community for first demonstrating to me the importance of listening to that still small voice. Joseph Campbell, who uttered those three magic words, "Follow your bliss," also served as a role model for this way of life.

Upon deciding to follow that bliss, I received invaluable assistance from my diligent and persevering agent Natasha Kern, and from my good friend and "West Coast editor" Ann Garrett. Forming a support group of other like-minded people has also been of tremendous value. Thanks go to the members of my AA (Artists Anonymous) support group—Ellie, Barbara, John, Dan.

I also wish to thank a number of people who believed in this project and helped to sustain it in the early stages—Kay David, Johanna F., Beverly Jensen, J. Martin Lasica, Corliss Lee, Amazonas Olivella, Daniel Peralta, Bonnie Schindler, Andrea Smith, and Martha Spice.

As with the book *Words That Heal*, Carol Schaeffer's proofreading and critical feedback proved invaluable.

Much of the material that comprises *Listening to Your Inner Voice* was taken from a series of workshops I gave and articles I wrote after the publication of *Words That Heal*. In this vein, I wish to thank the many Unity churches and the magazine editors, specifically Kathy Juline of *Science of*

Mind magazine, who gave me the opportunity to share my message.

Finally, I acknowledge and express gratitude to that indwelling spiritual presence that continues to guide and direct my way.

Let us be silent that we may hear the whispers of the gods.
Ralph Waldo Emerson

Listening to Your Inner Voice is a book of spiritual guidance that is designed to support you in tuning in to and acting upon your own inner wisdom.

As a spiritual being, you are connected to the intelligence that governs the Universe. By becoming still and listening to your inner voice, you can communicate with that indwelling presence and let it guide and direct your life.

Over the past few years, I have had the opportunity to teach the use of affirmations to thousands of individuals around the country and to observe this healing power at work. Since I consider affirmations such a useful tool in supporting the inner voice, I am continuing the direction I began in my previous book, *Words That Heal,* by presenting additional information on how to work with affirmations in your daily life.

While the format of *Listening to Your Inner Voice* closely follows that of *Words That Heal,* there exists a subtle difference in the underlying themes of the books' meditations. The inspiration for *Words That Heal* came to me during a difficult period in my life—I had just lost a home, job, and primary relationship. In order to respond to the despair I was facing, the words that came through me spoke of *hope, comfort,* and *support.*

By the time I started *Listening to Your Inner Voice*, I had emerged from the darkness and a new challenge presented itself. I asked, "Now that I am no longer preoccupied with the pain, what is my next step? How can I now get in touch with and fully express my purpose in life?" The essays of *Listening to Your Inner Voice* reflect this shift by speaking more to the issues of *individuality, purpose, guidance,* and *direction* than to those of pain and loss.

I like to think of this evolution as being analogous to the process of recovering from alcoholism. The first step is to stop drinking. Then, when sobriety is achieved, the real work of recovery can begin.

We are all in recovery—recovering from a sense of separation from our Source. When that separation is healed, we will no longer have to *listen* to our inner voice—we will *be it.* For now, may the words that follow help you to rediscover your connection to that Inner Light so that it can guide, direct, and make perfect your way.

Listening to Your Inner Voice

*To whatever degree you listen to and follow your intuition, you become
a creative channel for the higher power of the universe. When you
willingly follow where your creative energy leads, the higher power can
come through you to manifest its creative work. When this happens,
you will find yourself flowing with the energy, doing what you really
want to do, and feeling the power of the universe moving through you
to create or transform everything around you.*
Shakti Gawain

We live in a time of rapid transformation. The old
rules and guidelines are no longer valid. Everything is changing far too quickly. No longer can we turn to gurus or external teachers to provide the answers we seek. As we approach
the dawn of a new era, each of us is being called upon to listen to and be guided by the "still small voice" within.

In the course of this book, I will use the term *inner
voice* to describe that source of wisdom and knowing which
lies within us. The inner voice is known by many names—
the voice of intuition, the Higher Self, the God-self, the
Holy Spirit.

How to Develop Inner Listening

Over a century ago, Ralph Waldo Emerson stated,
"There is guidance for each of us, and by lowly listening we
shall hear the right words." The key to tapping the inner
voice lies in becoming quiet, stilling the mind, and allowing
intuition to bubble up into your awareness.

You can achieve this stillness through any process that relaxes you and slows down your thoughts—meditation, visualization, long walks, exercise, driving on a country road, etc. In the midst of this silence, your intuition will speak to you in any number of ways—through words, a bodily sensation, a gut feeling, a picture, or just a general sense about things. Be open to the way that is right for you. Trust your own response. In time and with practice, it will become clearer and easier to recognize.

Like all great spiritual truths, the idea of listening to yourself is simple in theory, but difficult in practice. This is because the higher voice is not the only voice seeking your attention. We have inside us a *false voice*, also known as the voice of the ego. While the inner voice gives expression to who we really are, the false voice focuses on who we think we should be. The inner voice supports our essential nature; the false voice denies it.

Each of these voices is accompanied by a number of clear signs. By recognizing these signs, we can learn to discern between the two.

Signs of the Inner Voice

The primary experience that emerges from listening to your inner voice is the presence of **inner peace**. This is the "peace of God, which passeth all understanding," an inner tranquility that emerges from a place deep in the soul. From this refuge, you can literally rise above any turmoil or chaos that surrounds you in the outer world.

The second sign that accompanies the inner voice is that of **joy**. The path of the spirit and the path of the **heart** are one and the same. When you go through life with an open heart, you are truly blessed. This is why mythologist Joseph Campbell advised his students, "Follow your bliss."

Following the inner voice also brings abundant **energy** and **vitality**. Have you ever wondered why certain people seem so enthusiastic and alive? Aligning ourselves with our Higher Power allows the life force to more easily flow through us.

Finally, you will be supported by **invisible hands**. There is no doubt about this. When you follow your heart's desire, life will support you. When you do your share, God will do His. When you reach out for what you want, the Universe will reach back and meet you halfway. Take a moment to review your life or the lives of your friends. You will find examples of how the Universe assists us when we are being faithful to the calling of the inner voice.

Signs of the False Voice

Just as the Universe provides clues when we follow the inner voice, it also lets us know when we follow the false voice. Following the false voice brings **anxiety** instead of peace, **burden** instead of joy, **judgment** instead of love, **confusion** instead of clarity, **blocks** instead of flow.

One of the key ways to recognize the voice of the ego is through the presence of **fear.** Going against family tradition, David dropped out of law school to pursue his passion for music. Initially, he felt a surge of joy and excitement as his authentic self came to the surface. Then suddenly a series of doubts flooded his awareness—"What if I fail?" "How will I get the money?" "What will people say?" This was the voice of FEAR speaking—fear of failure, fear of poverty, and fear of criticism.

Or perhaps you have just had an argument with your mate. You go within and the still small voice says, "Take the first step towards reconciliation." You feel a deep peace about this when suddenly the false voice pipes in, "It's too risky. What if I am rejected? I'm going to wait for the other person to reach out first."

Moreover, while the inner voice is committed to the truth, the false voice preaches dishonesty. Let's say that a bank has mistakenly credited you with a large sum of money. The ego says, "I don't have to report the error. They don't need the income as much as I do. I think I'll keep my mouth shut." These fearful words express a belief in scarcity—for me to have more, others must have less. The voice of love, on the other hand, lives in a consciousness of abundance. It says, "I gladly share what I have, for I know that there is enough to provide for all."

These voices can be further discerned by paying attention to the sensations in your body. For example, you might be trying to decide between two job opportunities. Become quiet and visualize each situation in your mind's eye. Pretend that you have begun working in each location, and then focus on your body's cues.

In seeing yourself in the first job, you may notice a heaviness or depression in the chest, rapid breathing, churning in the stomach, or some other sensation of discomfort.

The presence of these sensations is telling you that something is amiss.

In contemplating the second job, you may experience a warm sensation in the chest or stomach, a lightness in the heart, a feeling of enthusiasm, or a peace and tranquility. This is your spirit's way of telling you that the second job is a better choice.

Try experimenting with these cues until you find the ones that work for you. Over time, you will become skilled at discerning between the two voices and will choose the inner voice as the one to guide you.

Getting Off Track and How to Get Back On

What happens when we choose to follow the false voice? Consider the story of an elementary schoolteacher named Joan. At the beginning of the school year, she was offered a new teaching position. Although she was happy in her current classroom, the new job offered more money, responsibility, and prestige. "Maybe I *should* take it," she thought.

Immediately after accepting the position, Joan had a dream in which she was just barely holding on to the top ledge of a thirty-five-story skyscraper. As the week unfolded, her anxiety increased until she decided to become still, go inside, and ask for guidance. The inner voice responded loudly and clearly, telling her that she was not ready for the new job and needed to remain in her present position.

The next day, Joan nervously called her principal, fearing that she would be reprimanded for reneging on her contract. But her guidance did not let her down. The principal was understanding and said she would hire a different teacher. As Joan hung up the phone, a week's worth of tension dissolved from her body; she experienced a deep inner peace. Spirit was speaking.

This story illustrates a number of important principles. First, by listening to the voice of "should," Joan succumbed to the false voice. In almost all instances, the "should" voice represents a parental or societal message about obligation and duty. The inner voice, on the other hand, pursues a path for its own sake, for its own joy.

Second, Joan was able to turn her situation around because she used her pain as *feedback* to obtain a greater understanding of her situation. If she had denied or repressed her distress, it would have returned at a later point, perhaps as a physical illness. Ignoring the pain only creates more pain and leaves the original problem unsolved.

Third, Joan did not make the "wrong" decision. When we view every action as increasing our self-knowledge, there are no failures, only learning experiences. No matter what choice we make, we can grow through it if we remain open to the teaching that is presented.

Keys to Supporting the Inner Voice

At each moment in time, we are asked to make a choice—a choice between following the inner voice of truth or the false voice of separation. Here are some qualities that will help you to remain faithful to the highest that is within you:

courage—the ability to feel your fears and move forward in spite of them.

patience—the capacity to wait for your good and give yourself praise and acknowledgment, even when it is not coming from the world.

commitment—the willingness to do whatever it takes to pursue your vision, including the making of necessary sacrifices.

faith—the willingness to trust in an invisible means of support. At times you may be called to leave a known situation (a job, home, relationship, etc.) for the unknown. Your guidance may go against logic and reason. This is when you need the faith to *trust in the process*.

But here is the paradox. Those things we think of as secure exist in the world of form and are therefore subject to change. On the other hand, the one thing we think of as insubstantial, the world of spirit, is really the only secure place we have to stand. It is your connection to your spiritual nature, to your Higher Power, to God-in-you, that constitutes your real security, your ultimate grounding.

To summarize, in listening to your inner voice, you—

1) first ask for inner guidance;
2) then, get quiet and listen;
3) finally, act upon what you hear.

Step out in faith, and give life the opportunity to support you. If you keep your focus on that benevolent Higher Power, not only will you be guided, but also your life will unfold more beautifully than you ever could have imagined. The Universe will open doors for you that you did not even know existed! When Joseph Campbell left a prestigious university to pursue his passion for mythology, he had no idea that nearly sixty years later he would be sharing that passion with millions of people on television. But he trusted his intuition, took it a day at a time, and his life unfolded in perfect Divine order. The same can be true for you when you listen to and follow your inner voice.

Supporting Your Inner Voice through Affirmations

Healing the Beliefs That Bind You

*One discovers that destiny can be directed,
that one does not have to remain in bondage to the
first wax imprint made in childhood. One need not
be branded by the first pattern.
Once the deforming mirror is smashed, there is a
possibility of wholeness; there is a possibility of joy.*
Anais Nin

A necessary ingredient to staying true to the inner voice involves dealing with the fears, doubts, and worries that confront us whenever we go for what we want. Much of this resistance originates from the limiting messages that were communicated to us in our early childhood by parents, teachers, peers, relatives, television, religious training, and society as a whole. Although these external voices came from sources outside ourselves, we internalized them and made them our own. The task each of us faces is to go inside and decide which messages we want to accept and which we want to release.

Much of the time we are not even aware of this negative programming. But being unconscious about a belief or fear does not diminish its effect. On the contrary, a limiting belief will continue to work against you, even if you are unaware of its presence. What you don't know *can* hurt you!

A person who believes "there is not enough to go around" will remain lacking, no matter how hard he or she tries to prosper.

Before you can deal with a fear or limiting belief, you must first discover what it is. In order to escape from prison, you must realize that you are in prison. **Awareness,** therefore, is the first step to liberation.

One tool that is particularly helpful in creating this awareness is the affirmation—a positive thought or idea that you consciously focus on in order to achieve a desired result.[1] While affirmations are associated with "positive thinking," they also provide a way to (1) *uncover* and (2) *release* old and limiting beliefs. Let's explore the process in detail.

[1] Those readers who are not familiar with affirmations will find an introduction to them in Appendix A.

Step 1: Become Aware of Your Limiting Beliefs

To become aware of the beliefs that bind you, choose an area of your life that feels incomplete or lacking in some way. It is here that your limiting beliefs are most strongly operating.

Next, decide what you want to occur in that area of life. Ask yourself, "What would it be like if this part of my life were whole?" Use your imagination to see, feel, and hear the result you are seeking.

Finally, create an affirmation, a positive statement in the first person and the present tense, that states the result you are seeking. Here are some sample affirmations:

Area of Lack	Healing Affirmation
Self-Esteem	I love and accept myself the way I am.
Relationships	I am attracting open and loving relationships.
Creativity	I am in touch with my passion.
Work/Career	I feel great about what I do for a living.
Prosperity	I have more than I need, and so I share with my world.
Health	The cells of my body radiate with vitality.
School	I feel good about my goals

11

| Spiritual Development | All things are working together for good in my life. |

After you have created your affirmation, you can use it to bring your limiting beliefs into the light of day. In the book *Words That Heal,* I introduced a dialogue technique which I have since expanded and named the "Affirmation-Dialogue Process." Briefly, it works as follows:

Divide a sheet of paper into *three* columns. Label the left-hand column "Affirmation," the middle column "First Response," and the third column "Second Response."

Then, after getting into a relaxed and receptive state of mind, write your affirmation in the left-hand column. Afterwards, be still and notice what bubbles up from the subconscious mind. In the "first response" column, write down your response, no matter how irrelevant it may appear. The process is similar to free association.

Repeat the process until you have noted all the responses that come to your awareness. When you have finished, the middle column will most likely contain a list of the major negative beliefs and assumptions you hold regarding this affirmation.

Patricia applied the affirmation-dialogue process to a therapeutic process known as "inner child work"—the process of communicating with the child that lives inside us and giving it the love and support it needs. To reinforce her ability to nurture and love this part of her personality, Patricia created the affirmation, "I can be a nurturing parent to my inner child."

Affirmation	First Response	Second Response
I can be a nurturing parent to my inner child.	You <u>are</u> a child.	
I can be a nurturing parent to my inner child.	You have no control.	
I can be a nurturing parent to my inner child.	You can't do anything right.	
I can be a nurturing parent to my inner child.	You are going to fail.	
I can be a nurturing parent to my inner child.	You will probably abandon it.	
I can be a nurturing parent to my inner child.	She isn't safe with you.	

I feel good about
my career goals

I fear the
loss of current
financial
stability

⊥⊥

⟶ I really do !

13

Step 2: Release Those Beliefs

As you can see, Patricia is engaged in a conversation, perhaps *argument* is the more accurate term, with herself. The dispute pits the *inner voice*, symbolized by the affirmation, against the *external voices* of her negative programming and conditioning. The affirmation says YES to the inner voice; the negative beliefs respond NO!

The essence of the dialogue can be represented as follows:

Affirmation	What Comes Up
Yes	No
Yes	No
Yes	No

Now that the affirmation-dialogue process has made Patricia conscious of her negative beliefs, the next step is to change those no's into yes's so that *what she wants* (the conscious mind) and *what she believes she deserves* (the subconscious mind) can be in total agreement.

Affirmation	What Comes Up
Yes	Yes
Yes	Yes
Yes	Yes

This is the function of the "second response," which provides the opportunity to immediately respond to the external or "no" voice and set the record straight. There are two advantages to this approach. Since a lie left unchallenged will eventually assume the aura of truth, quickly responding to the "no" diminishes its power and validity. In addition, replacing the "no" voice with a positive statement makes it less likely that the former will return. If you are a visual person, you can erase the negative picture or scene in your mind's eye and replace it with a positive one.

Let us return to Patricia. Having uncovered her negative beliefs in the middle column, she can go back and review them one at a time. In each case she can ask herself, "Is there anything that I have to say in response to this statement? Are there any misperceptions or falsehoods that I would like to clear up? Do I wish to set the record straight?"

As Patricia answers each misperception with the truth about herself, she will write her reply in the "second response" column, directly opposite the statement it is meant to replace. The following dialogue shows how she responded to each of her limiting beliefs.

Affirmation	First Response	Second Response
I can be a nurturing parent to my inner child.	You <u>are</u> a child.	I am also an adult.
I can be a nurturing parent to my inner child.	You have no control.	I have gained control over many areas of my life.

I can be a nurturing parent to my inner child.	You can't do anything right.	Not true. I have accomplished a great deal.
I can be a nurturing parent to my inner child.	You are going to fail.	I am going to succeed.
I can be a nurturing parent to my inner child.	You will probably abandon it.	I can change.
I can be a nurturing parent to my inner child.	She isn't safe with you.	She is safe most of the time.

Patricia was clearly empowered by confronting her negative beliefs and replacing them with the truth about herself. As a final step in this process, she took a number of statements from the "second response" column and brought them together to create a cohesive declaration of the good she is seeking. Her example reads as follows:

"I can be a nurturing parent to my inner child. As an adult, I have gained control over many areas of my life. I have accomplished a great deal and am going to succeed now. I can change my old patterns. My inner child is safe in my hands."

Upon reading these words to herself each day, Patricia will further reinforce the power of the original affirmation.

When working with the affirmation-dialogue process, let your intuition be your guide. You don't have to refute every statement in the middle column. Just respond where it feels appropriate. Experience how empowering it feels to give yourself the support you deserve. You'll be amazed at how quickly you can release or transmute old beliefs when you end the internal dialogue on an affirmative note.

Now matter how strong your conditioning may be, it is possible to transmute your negative beliefs into positive ones. You do not have to remain the victim of your past programming or conditioning. There is a way out. Your inner voice is waiting to guide you into the fullness of joy, once you release the beliefs that bind you.

Revelations from the Unconscious

Behold, I show you a mystery, we shall not all sleep, but we shall all be changed. In a moment, in the twinkling of an eye, at the last trump: for the trumpet shall sound . . . and we shall all be changed.
I Corinthians 15:51

We have seen that using the affirmation-dialogue process works to bring one's core negative beliefs to the surface where they can be released or transformed. Yet not all the material lying outside the realm of conscious awareness is negative. In many instances, the affirmation-dialogue process will reveal those aspects of our **higher wisdom** and **intuition** that can shed light on a significant problem or issue we are facing.

For example, an aspiring professional golfer decided to create an affirmation to heal her smoking habit. This is what occurred as she wrote down the affirmation and listened for the response.

Affirmation	First Response
I am a nonsmoker.	I'll gain weight.
I am a nonsmoker.	It's one of the few pleasures I have left.
I am a nonsmoker.	It's too hard to stop.
I am a nonsmoker.	<u>Smoking gives me an excuse for not giving 100 percent to life.</u>

At this point, the woman bolted upright and exclaimed, "Where did that come from?!" Suddenly she realized that the real issue was not her smoking, but her fear of functioning at full capacity. To get to the root of that fear, she created a new affirmation, "I am now giving 100 percent to life." This is what followed.

Affirmation	First Response
I am now giving 100 percent to life.	I'm afraid I'll fall short.
I am now giving 100 percent to life.	I'm not good enough.
I am now giving 100 percent to life.	Nothing I do is ever right.

When she finished, I asked her if she had ever been criticized as a child. "Everything I did was put down. I was never right," she replied. Here, then, was the problem. Her *fear of criticism and disapproval* was the true cause of her lack of participation in life. Smoking was merely a symptom.

The significance of this type of breakthrough cannot be overstated. Like peeling the layers of an onion, the affirmation-dialogue process allows one to go deeper and deeper until the core of the problem is at last revealed.

For example, Michael used the following affirmation to support his desire to attract a new relationship.

Affirmation	First Response
I now have a satisfying relationship with my ideal mate.	Why should it work this time?
I now have a satisfying relationship with my ideal mate.	The odds are against it.
I now have a satisfying relationship with my ideal mate.	I haven't let go of my ex-wife, yet.

At this point, Michael abruptly put down his pen. Until now, he had considered himself fully healed from a painful divorce. But the last response made it clear that he was still holding on to his former spouse.

Here is another affirmation that led to a similarly important insight.

Affirmation	First Response
I have good relationships with people, money, work, and God.	I try so hard. I deserve to have good relationships in these areas.
I have good relationships with people, money, work, and God.	I work very hard at creating good relationships. They should be perfect.

I have good relationships with people, money, work, and God.	Maybe I'm working too hard at all of this.
I have good relationships with people, money, work, and God.	Wait a minute. I am working too hard. I need to create a new affirmation.

Which he did. Michael's new affirmation read, "In my relationships with people, money, work, and God, it's okay to rest, relax, and have fun." What needed affirming was the desire to relax and let go, not the desire for perfect relationships.

Here is a final example. A man suffering from anxiety attacks created the affirmation "I am calm and peaceful."

Affirmation	First Response
I am calm and peaceful.	Says who?
I am calm and peaceful.	I don't feel that way.
I am calm and peaceful.	<u>Why haven't I opened my boat business yet?</u>

Suddenly, this man realized that his lack of peace was caused by the suppression of a long-standing dream. Although he hadn't thought about the idea in years, his unconscious was telling him that now was the time to pursue it.

21

Subsequently, he began to affirm the new business. With the help of the affirmation-dialogue process, he faced and dealt with his fears of failure instead of running from them as he had done in the past.

These examples clearly demonstrate that the inner voice of truth and guidance is continually beckoning to be heard. The affirmation-dialogue process provides a simple structure that invites our higher knowing to speak to us through spontaneous insights and breakthroughs. Using affirmations in your daily life will help you learn to recognize these messages of truth as they arise.

Creating a Daily Ritual

Although the affirmation-dialogue process is a powerful technique, it needs to be practiced to derive the full benefits. I have found it helpful to create a daily ritual or practice in which one sets aside a short period of time to work with the affirmations. What follows is a description of this process.

Get into a comfortable position and close your eyes. You may wish to play some quiet music in the background, or you can bask in the silence. When you are relaxed, ask yourself, "What particular issue do I want to focus on at this moment? What do I need to become aware of right now?" Then pay attention to whatever pops into your consciousness.

After choosing your topic (work, relationships, health, prosperity, creativity, etc.), compose an affirmation that expresses the outcome you are seeking. The affirmation can be one that you are already working with or it could be a new one that you formulate.

Once you have decided on the affirmation, begin working with the affirmation-dialogue process. Write the affirmation in the left-hand column and then write down what comes up in the "first response" column. After completing the list, decide if you wish to challenge any of the negative statements. Write these replies in the "second response" column.

Allow the process to take you where it will. Be open to the affirmation changing form or turning into an entirely new affirmation. Let your inner wisdom guide you as you write. Notice the insights and understandings you gain as you connect with your inner knowing.

When you feel that you have come to the end of your session, give thanks to your inner voice for communicating with you. Experience how empowering it is to give yourself the support you deserve.

People often ask, "How much time should I spend with my affirmation?" In most cases, fifteen to twenty minutes is sufficient. Even if you have only ten minutes to spare, you will start to see results. Over time your affirmations will take on a life of their own, transforming your reality according to the words you have spoken.

It is often said that the most elementary forces in the Universe are the most powerful. The affirmation-dialogue process is a simple technique that puts you in touch with your inner voice and brings to awareness what you need for your spiritual growth.

In a very real sense, affirmations empower us to become our own healers.

The Main Text

Let the words of my mouth and the meditation of my heart
be acceptable in Thy sight, O Lord,
my strength and my redeemer.
Psalm 19:14

Instructions for Using the Main Text

At each moment in time, we are asked to make a choice—a choice between following the higher voice of love or the ego's voice of fear and doubt. The fifty-two inspirational meditations that follow offer thoughts and reflections that are designed to directly support and empower that higher voice.

Each of these meditations is also complemented by:

• A series of **Affirmations**—positive thoughts and ideas that when repeated will help you reinforce your inner voice as well as transform your negative beliefs and attitudes. For those readers not familiar with affirmations, Appendix A provides an overview of what affirmations are and how to use them.

• A **Quotation** that encapsulates the essence of the teaching.

You can turn to these fifty-two passages on a daily or weekly basis, or whenever you feel the need for direction or support.

Selecting a Passage

When you are ready to choose a passage, place yourself in a comfortable spot in your environment. If you make a habit of meditating, you can use your normal meditation area. Otherwise, find a space where you will not be disturbed.

Next, turn to a meditation. People have found various ways of accessing the text. Here are a few ideas to consider:

1) Start with the first meditation and read the rest in order. Since there are fifty-two in all, you can focus on one for each week of the year.

2) Look through the Table of Contents and choose a theme that directly speaks to you.

3) Open the book at random, and read what is in front of you.

The last method, called dowsing, is my favorite. I find that I invariably turn to the teaching that is just perfect for me. Try it and see what happens!

Now glance at the **meditation, affirmations**, and **quotation**. They were designed to function as a whole unit so you can read them in order. Or perhaps one section will especially appeal to you. Let your intuition be your guide, drawing to you whatever words you need to hear.

You may wish to write down any insights in a separate notebook or journal. If you are inspired to create your own affirmations, you can record them in the space provided in this book or in a journal you keep.

Let us begin the exciting and transforming journey of listening to your inner voice. May the words that follow support you to stay on your very own path and remain true to the highest and best that is within you.

ONE

To Dream Is to Be Practical

Recently a filmmaker friend approached me with good news. He had just received a grant to do a documentary. "I can't believe it," he said. "I'm finally getting paid for my work. I can't believe how lucky I am to be doing this."

After our conversation, I thought: "This person believes that he is earning a living **in spite of doing** what he loves; but the reality is just the opposite. It is **because** he is following his passion that he prospers. As he aligns himself with his higher purpose, the Universe cannot help but make straight, smooth, and perfect his way."

People who say, "Be practical," don't realize that following your heart is the most practical thing one can do. There is no greater way to ensure success than being true to who you are. On the other hand, there is nothing more likely to block that success than turning away from your calling. Living at cross-purposes with your true nature creates struggle and lack of fulfillment at a deep level. It is hard to be someone other than yourself.

The lesson is clear: As impractical as it may sound, the safest and most secure way to lead your life is to follow your dream.

Affirmations

1. I advance confidently in the direction of my dreams.

2. I am grateful for having found my calling.

3. God does great things through me.

4. By following my heart, I prosper.

5. I have wonderful work in a wonderful way; I give wonderful service for wonderful pay.

6. *Your own* _____

_____

_____ ❦ _____

Words to Consider
*If one advances confidently in the direction of his dreams
and endeavors to live the life which he has imagined,
he will meet with a success unexpected in common hours.*
Henry David Thoreau

TWO

Your Life Is Your Art

A short time ago, a friend handed me the following credo. It read:

This is the artist's dream:
To receive the inspiration to create,
To share that creation with others,
And to be totally supported in the process.

I asked him to explain further. "It all begins with inspiration," he said, "an inspiration that calls us to create. Once the inspiration is received, then we can bring that vision into the world as a song, painting, book, invention, new business—or any other tangible form.

"After the creation is born, it needs to be shared with others. No one creates in a vacuum. It is only when the vision is successfully communicated to its intended audience that it truly comes alive.

"Finally, the artist needs to be supported for what he does. If he has made a positive connection with his audience, the support will come—financially and emotionally. And while it may not always be there immediately, it will ultimately arrive. This is where the artist needs to trust and be patient."

This dream is not just the artist's dream. It is our dream as well. Through work or play, job or family, vocation or avocation, you can experience the joy of creating, sharing, and being acknowledged. Experience this creative process and you will never grow old in spirit. Have you ever known an artist or dreamer who "retired"?

Affirmations

1. I am receiving the inspiration to create—and am able to carry it out.

2. I am joyfully *sharing* my creations with others.

3. I have a dream.

4. I am drawing to myself the people, circumstances, and finances that will make my dream come true.

5. My work is love in action.

6. *Your own* _____
   _____

——————— ❦ ———————

Words to Consider
*What we lack are not scientists but poets and people
to reveal to the heart
what the heart is ready to receive.*
Joseph Campbell

THREE

To Thine Own Self Be True

"To thine own self be true." "Live the life you were meant to live." "Be the person you were meant to be." These statements convey a wonderful truth—that when we go inside and trust our intuition, life opens before us. When we ignore our inner leanings, however, trouble arises.

Joe had a love of the outdoors; but like his father, he became addicted to his work. Though he built up a successful law practice, Joe felt creatively stifled and inwardly desolate. One day Joe was diagnosed with an inoperable brain tumor. Realizing he had nothing to lose, he decided to pursue his passion and hike the Pacific Crest trail. Six months later, the tumor had disappeared.

Trying to live out somebody else's life script is like putting a size 10 foot into a size 7 shoe. The size simply does not fit. No matter how hard you force yourself to adjust to your situation, the discomfort continues.

Why not start off with the right fit? Acknowledge your unique gifts and talents, as well as your wants and needs. Then seek out situations and circumstances that will allow them their full expression. This route may take time, but the results are worth it: a life of peace and fulfillment that comes from being true to yourself.

Affirmations

1. I am actualizing the highest and best that is within me.

2. I am true to myself.

3. Being honest with myself helps me to be honest with others.

4. I give myself the freedom to discover and pursue my own path.

5. I march to the beat of my own drum—and create wonderful music.

6. *Your own* _____

_____

Words to Consider
And this above all, to thine own self be true.
And it must follow as night the day,
thou canst not be false to any man.
Shakespeare

FOUR

The True Treasure

Consider the following story of misplaced priorities. While hiking in the wilderness, I met a man whose T-shirt carried the following message: "He who dies with the most toys, wins."

As I pondered those words, I was sure that the author meant the opposite of what he said. No one on his deathbed ever stated, "I wish I had spent more time at the office." We were put on this earth not to accumulate "toys," but to reap the gifts of the spirit. These gifts come to us when we dedicate our lives to something greater than ourselves—a path of service in the world, the raising of a loving family, the creation of beauty through art, or any passion that inspires one.

Having lived in this manner, you can look back over your life with a real sense of fulfillment. By following the path of peace, love, and joy, you will discover your true treasure—one that transcends death itself.

He who dies, having followed his heart, wins.

Affirmations

1. Joy is my compass.

2. As I follow the path of my heart, I discover my true treasure.

3. I release my unnecessary attachments to people, things, or situations in the world.

4. My spiritual growth is my top priority.

5. When I am being true to the highest and best in me, the rest of my life falls into place.

6. *Your own* _____

_____

Words to Consider

Lay not up for yourselves treasures on earth where moth and dust doth corrupt, where thieves break through and steal; but lay up treasures in heaven . . . for where your treasure is, there will be your heart also.
Matthew 6:19–21

FIVE

Living Your Priorities

Here is a simple way to get in touch with your priorities. Imagine that you have an incurable illness and are given six months to live. As the doctors inform you of their findings, see yourself accepting your imminent mortality with the resolve, *"I am going to spend the last months of my life living to the fullest, doing those things that are truly important to me."* Then imagine yourself living out those six months in the manner in which you have decided.

Afterwards, note your experience. During your remaining days, what did you do, who did you see, and where did you go? What do these choices say about what is really important to you—your values and priorities? Are you living them today? If you are not, you may want to learn from Tony's story.

After being diagnosed with AIDS, Tony decided to embrace life. He bought a house, planted a garden, and nurtured his important relationships. As a result, he lived the remaining three years of his life in pure joy.

The tragedy is that his life ended just as he was beginning to live. Why wait for a life-threatening experience to motivate you to take action? Confront your fears and pursue what brings you happiness and joy. There is no better time than now.

Affirmations

1. I am in touch with my priorities, and I act on them.

2. By living each day as if it were my last, I experience the fullness of life.

3. I am fully and freely expressing who I am.

4. I release whatever fears are holding me back.

5. I have the courage to take risks.

6. *Your own* _____
   _____

———————— ❦ ————————

Words to Consider
Whatever you can do or dream you can, begin it.
Boldness has genius, power and magic in it. Begin it now.
Goethe

SIX

Finding Your Purpose

Everyone has a dream. Everyone has a purpose or mission, something specific he is called to do. You are on this earth for a reason. Although you can temporarily hide from yourself, you can never lose your connection to your purpose. It is *always* with you, beckoning to be uncovered. You just need to listen and let it speak to you.

When you do decide to follow your dream, be prepared for resistance. The old beliefs and messages from the past that say it cannot be done will come rushing to the surface. How will you respond to these voices of fear and doubt? Will you allow them to immobilize you? Or will you tell them who is in charge and move forward in spite of your fears?

Despite the objections of everyone around her, Augusta pursued her dream of becoming an Olympic track athlete. At first a series of disappointing performances seemed to confirm the predictions of her family and friends. But then she won a race. The improvement continued until a number of first-place finishes gave her a spot on the Olympic team.

No matter what the obstacles, choose to be true to your purpose and let it guide and direct your way. Your destiny is beckoning you. It is time to heed the call.

Affirmations

1. I am aligned with my higher purpose.

2. I am in touch with my destiny.

3. I hear my inner voice and heed the call.

4. I am living a life of purpose and passion.

5. I follow my dreams and make them reality.

6. *Your own* _____

_____

❦

Words to Consider
*The reasonable man encounters circumstances
and adapts himself to them.
The unreasonable man persists in trying
to adapt circumstances to himself.
All progress depends upon the unreasonable man.*
George Bernard Shaw

SEVEN

Not by Bread Alone

The other day I was feeling off center, and so I took a walk around the block to lift my spirits. As I passed one of the neighbor's homes, I spotted a luxury car and began to imagine my pleasure at owning and driving such a vehicle. Suddenly, a still small voice whispered from within, "You can't fill a spiritual void with a physical object. Because you are a spiritual being living in a material world, your deeper needs for love and connectedness can never be satisfied in purely material terms."

And yet we climb the ladder of material success only to discover that it is leaning against the wrong wall. It is clear that human beings need a certain amount of food, clothing, shelter, and comfort to meet their physical needs. But anything beyond that is not truly essential for inner contentment. As the philosopher Marcus Aurelius said, *"Very little is needed to make a happy life."*

In Scripture we read, "Man does not live by bread alone, but by every word that proceeds out of the mouth of God." Ask yourself, "What are my spiritual and emotional needs, and what steps am I taking to address them?" As you begin to feed and nourish yourself with spiritual food, your soul's hunger will be filled. There is no deeper satisfaction than this.

Affirmations

1. I nourish my soul with what it needs.

2. I know what is truly important in my life.

3. The love of my friends and family defines my true riches.

4. My physical needs are more than met, and I give thanks for this.

5. I am peaceful and content at a deep level of my being.

6. *Your own* _____

    _____

———————— ❧ ————————

Words to Consider
Contentment makes poor men rich,
Discontent makes rich men poor.
Benjamin Franklin

Life Is for Giving

When Albert Schweitzer said, "The only ones of you who will be truly happy are those who have found and learned how to serve," he was stating an ancient truth—that the meaning of life lies in giving. The quality of your life is in direct proportion to your willingness to give.

In the classic movie *It's a Wonderful Life*, George Bailey discovered this truth. Though he had many opportunities to pursue his ambitions elsewhere, George remained in his community and dedicated himself to providing affordable housing to its members. When his guardian angel showed him what the town would be like if he had never been born, Bailey realized how much of a difference his giving had made.

George also discovered another secret—that what you give is what you receive. Whatever you give out comes back to you. When you extend yourself to nurture the spiritual growth of another, you nurture your own growth. Although his material possessions were modest, George Bailey was toasted the "richest" (i.e., the most beloved) man in town by the people of Bedford Falls. Later he remarked, "No man can be poor as long as he has friends."

Bailey gave of himself for the joy of giving, and joy is what he received. By following this path, we, too, can be blessed.

Affirmations

1. Freely I give; freely I receive.

2. I give for its own sake, because it feels right in my heart.

3. Giving is its own reward.

4. As I love well, I live well.

5. All that I give, I give to myself.

6. *Your own* _____

Words to Consider
*It is one of the most beautiful compensations of this life
that no man can sincerely try to help another
without also helping himself.*
Ralph Waldo Emerson

What Will I Leave Behind?

As we grow older and face our own mortality, we begin to ask ourselves, "After I am gone, will my life have made a difference? What will I leave behind?" One way to contribute to future generations is through art. The Latin proverb states, "Ars longa, vita brevis" (life is brief but art endures). Centuries after his death, a writer, painter, or musician still speaks to us through his creations.

Acts of committed service also open the doors to immortality. As Martin Luther King, Jr., prophetically stated two weeks before his death, "I won't have much money to leave behind. I won't have the finer things in life to leave behind. I just want to leave a committed life behind."

Not everyone is required to make a sacrifice of Dr. King's magnitude, but all contributions have their impact. *Whatever* we give in loving service is what we leave behind. In the words of Thomas Stanley, "To leave the world a little bit better, whether by a healthy child, a garden patch, or a redeemed social condition; to know that even one life has breathed easier because you have lived: This is to have succeeded."

Affirmations

1. My life has a purpose and a meaning.

2. I have found something to live for.

3. I dedicate myself to a worthwhile endeavor.

4. Though my existence is finite, my ability to love is infinite.

5. What I give in love shall endure forever.

6. *Your own* _____
   _____

_____ _____

Words to Consider
If you want to leave something behind,
plant a tree, have children, or write a book.
The Talmud

TEN

All Assignments Are Equal

As each of us gets in touch with the specific ways to serve, it is tempting to judge the importance of our work by comparing it to someone else's achievements. And when that person or group earns more money, receives more praise and recognition, or influences more people, our efforts may feel diminished in stature.

But the truth of the matter is that the spiritual path is not a "numbers game." Ways of serving cannot be compared to one another. In spirit's eyes, each mission is just as important as the next. All assignments are equal.

A director of a school for emotionally handicapped children says about her work, "My job is to serve with joy and to let spirit work through me. It is up to God, not me, to determine how many kids I actually reach. Ultimately, the numbers are not important; for if only one soul's life has been changed through this work, it has been worth it."

Like this woman, your job is to discover what your purpose is—and then fulfill it. It does not matter how small your contribution may seem. You have a special part to play that no one else can duplicate. In God's eyes, all assignments are equal.

Affirmations

1. I appreciate and acknowledge myself for the contribution I am making.

2. I appreciate and acknowledge others for the contributions they are making.

3. I am exactly where I need to be.

4. I am guided by spirit to my divinely designed calling.

5. I find intrinsic pleasure and satisfaction in the work I do.

6. *Your own* _____

_____

——————— ❧ ———————

Words to Consider
*Look for your own. Do not do what someone else could do
as well as you. Care for nothing in yourself but what you
feel exists nowhere else —and out of yourself create . . .
that most irreplaceable of beings.*
André Gide

ELEVEN

The Divine Partnership

There exists a Divine partnership between God and man that is wonderfully depicted in the following story. A young minister was driving through the countryside when he spotted a farmer tilling 40 acres of magnificent farmland. The minister pulled over and addressed the farmer, "God has certainly blessed you with a wonderful piece of land." The farmer replied, "Yes, but you should have seen the mess it was in when God had it to Himself!"

A well-known entrepreneur was asked the secret of her business success. She answered, "I pray as if everything depends on God, but act as if everything depends on me." It is not enough just to pray for and affirm our good. Like the farmer and businesswoman, we must also take concrete steps to make our dreams a reality.

Working together, we and spirit form an unbeatable combination. Neither can succeed without the other. Just as nature provided the land but needed the farmer to till the soil, spirit needs us to bring about heaven on earth. Let us work together as Divine partners to fulfill this promise.

Affirmations

1. I see myself in partnership with the Infinite.

2. When I do my share, God does His.

3. As I take responsibility for my life, the Universe answers my requests.

4. As I follow my bliss, I attract whatever support I need.

5. Working with spirit, all things become possible.

6. Your own _____

_____

❧

Words to Consider
Pray to God but row to shore.
Proverb

TWELVE

Persistence

Consider these words of Calvin Coolidge: "Nothing in the world can take the place of persistence. Talent will not; nothing is more common than unsuccessful men with talent. Genius will not; unrewarded genius is almost a proverb. Education will not; the world is filled with educated derelicts. Persistence and determination are alone omnipotent. 'Press on!' has been and always will be the answer to every human problem."

Coolidge was right. In the successful pursuit of a vision, persistence always makes the difference. Colonel Sanders approached 1,094 restaurants before he found someone who would try his recipe for fried chicken. Thomas Edison made over 2,000 attempts before he invented the light bulb. Abraham Lincoln failed in two businesses and lost five elections before he became president.

The ability to persevere in the face of adversity takes a special kind of faith. It's easy to get discouraged when obstacles appear. If you are in such a situation, know that time is on your side. *Time* plus sustained *effort* always produce results. After waiting thirty-three years to win the world championship, a coach was asked, "Was it worth the wait?" "Absolutely," he replied. "In fact, the long delay actually made the victory sweeter."

Affirmations

1. I am patient and persevering.

2. Every setback makes me more determined to reach my goal.

3. My persistence and determination work miracles.

4. My greatest glory is in rising every time I fall.

5. With every delay, there's a blessing on its way.

6. *Your own* _____

_____

————————  ————————

Words to Consider
A big shot is just a little shot who kept on shooting.
Zig Ziglar

THIRTEEN

The Power of a Made-up Mind

Life responds not to what we wish or even to what we desire. Life responds to a made-up mind. The moment that you definitely commit yourself, then the Universe moves, too. Doors open for you that normally would have remained closed. A whole stream of events unfolds which leads to the desired outcome.

One Christmas, a woman wanted to take her children to see a performance of *The Nutcracker* ballet. Unfortunately, she did not have the money to purchase the tickets. Nonetheless, she was totally committed to seeing the show. She visualized the outcome and affirmed that she would attend that evening's performance. Two hours before the show, a friend who worked as a tour guide called. He had just arrived in town to see *The Nutcracker* with his tour, but three clients could not attend. Would she and her children like to go?

Many would call this coincidence. Those who understand the workings of the Divine mind know that the woman's 100 percent intention to be at the show drew to her the good that she desired. The same can be true for you once you employ the power of a made-up mind.

Affirmations

1. I now tap the power of a made-up mind.

2. I choose my goals and commit to them wholeheartedly.

3. When I make up my mind, the Universe moves to support me.

4. I believe in my dream.

5. My momentum is increasing every day.

6. *Your own* _____

———————— ❦ ————————

Words to Consider
There is nothing more potent than thought.
Deed follows word and word follows thought.
And where the thought is mighty and pure,
the result is mighty and pure.
Gandhi

FOURTEEN

Discipline

It is no accident that the words *discipline* and *disciple* come from the same root. To be a disciple of any path, one must be disciplined. Life works best when we learn to discipline ourselves.

Discipline *liberates* rather than confines you. Discipline allows you to function with ease and grace. After years of practicing his strokes, a tennis player can hit the ball without having to think about it. What once took conscious effort is now second nature.

Unfortunately, many of us had discipline forced upon us as children. Naturally, we rebelled against an externally imposed structure. We were not shown that true discipline always comes from within, and the motivation for that urge is *love*. When we are doing what we love, when we are pursuing something that has meaning, discipline becomes natural. As one Olympic athlete explained, "I don't mind working out every day. Because I love what I am doing, my training is not a burden but a joy."

Discipline is your ticket to freedom and path to excellence. Choose to be disciplined in all your endeavors and become the master of yourself and your life.

Affirmations

1. I lovingly do what it takes to support the achievement of my goals.

2. Discipline is my ticket to freedom.

3. I do what it takes to do what I love.

4. I make excellent use of my time.

5. I reward myself for my efforts on a daily basis.

6. *Your own* _____

_____

———————— ❦ ————————

Words to Consider
*My father taught me that only through self-discipline
can you achieve freedom.
Pour water into a cup and you can drink.
Without the cup, the water would splash over. The cup is discipline.*
Ricardo Montalban

FIFTEEN

It Is Better to Light a Candle

With all the negativity that surrounds us, it is easy to become overwhelmed. It is also tempting to fight against the negative or to declare war on it. Yet a master teacher offered a better way: "Resist not evil, but overcome evil with good."

Imagine you are in a dark room. Wanting the darkness to leave, you curse and fight against it. But no matter how much effort you make, the darkness remains. Turn on the light switch, however, and the night vanishes in an instant.

In a similar manner, when the light of truth is shed on a situation, fear and disharmony dissolve. When you send out a positive thought to another person or take a constructive action, an enormous amount of good is accomplished. Each good act begets another until a network of love and light is created.

The purpose of life is to reflect this light into places that are dark. Let your light shine and stay focused on the power of love. When enough of us have turned on our spiritual light switches, the earth will become as bright as a shining star. Where, then, could darkness dwell?

Affirmations

1. I focus on the positive.

2. Rather than being against hatred, I am for love.

3. I look for the good in each situation.

4. I am a person who seeks solutions.

5. Every problem I encounter contains a gift.

6. *Your own* _____
   _____

_____ ❦ _____

Words to Consider
It is better to light a candle than to curse the darkness.
Chinese Proverb

SIXTEEN

Courage

Without courage it is virtually impossible to progress along the spiritual path. Courage enables us to face the fears that arise when we go for what we want.

Courage often involves going against conventional wisdom and walking the path alone. It takes courage to give up the high-paying job and work part time while you start your own business on the side. It takes courage to leave an unworkable relationship. It takes courage to face the pain of one's childhood and seek to heal it. In short, it takes courage to be oneself.

People ask, "How can I have courage when I'm afraid?" The answer is clear. Courage is not the absence of fear, but the willingness to move forward in spite of it. When fear comes up in your life, fully feel and experience it. If you try to push it away, it will only expand.

Say to your fear, "I acknowledge you. But as I connect with my higher knowing, I see that you are not in alignment with my true calling. Because I have the courage and the faith to follow my heart, I am moving ahead with my plans in spite of you." Then proceed. Like the actor whose stage fright leaves in the first moments of the play, yours will fade as you actively embrace your own unique destiny—with courage.

Affirmations

1. I listen to and follow my inner voice.

2. I feel my fear and proceed anyway.

3. I act to please myself rather than others.

4. I courageously move forward in the direction of my dreams.

5. I am true to myself.

6. *Your own* _____
_____

—————— ❧ ——————

Words to Consider
"Come to the edge," he said. "No, we will fall," they replied.
They came to the edge. He pushed them . . . and they flew.
Apollinaire

SEVENTEEN

Claim Your Inheritance

Throughout spiritual traditions, human beings are depicted as the children of a loving Creator who has offered us His kingdom. Repeatedly we hear that abundance, joy, and prosperity are at hand *right now*. Yet, though the harvest is here, "the laborers are few." Why is this so?

In spiritual life there exists a law called the **law of demand and supply.** Before substance can manifest itself, a need must be expressed. For example, if I desire to buy a home, this "demand" creates a force of attraction that will draw my home to me. The request comes first, the demonstration, second. If you do not ask, you will not receive.

Many factors limit what we are willing to ask for. We tell ourselves, "I don't deserve it; I'm not good enough." "How can I succeed when others have failed before me?" "Why should I have when others do not?"

In order to harvest the fields of plenty, we must plow up and discard these weeds of unworthiness, doubt, and guilt. Such self-imposed beliefs block the good that is our rightful gift. Affirm your own worthiness to partake of life's bountiful harvest. Then go forth to claim your Divine inheritance.

Affirmations

1. I am a child of God, and therefore deserve all of God's good.

2. I release any feelings of unworthiness that keep out the good.

3. I go forth to claim my Divine inheritance of love, health, success, and prosperity.

4. As my cup runs over, I share my blessings with all whom I meet.

5. I open to receive.

6. *Your own* _____

_____

_____ ❧ _____

Words to Consider
Ask and it shall be given to you. Seek and ye shall find. Knock and the door shall be opened. For everyone who asks receives, and he who seeks finds, and to him who knocks, it shall be opened.
Matthew 7:7–8

EIGHTEEN

Let the Power Work through You

The times that life works best are when we get out of the way and let the power work through us. The writer says of an inspired short story, "I didn't write this story; it seemed to write itself." After a record-breaking performance an athlete recalls, "I just had an 'on' day. My shots kept falling in."

Each of us has had moments when we felt as if we were riding the crest of a wave or were being pushed from behind by a gentle wind. The more you can surrender to the universal energy and go with its flow, the easier life becomes.

Compare this experience to that of trying to control and manipulate life through the limited ego. Everything becomes a strain and an effort, a constant struggle. We tire easily. By the time we cross the finish line, we wonder if the race was worth running.

A better way is stated by the paradox, "You give it all up to have it all." Whatever your current situation, step back and let the power work through you. You'll be amazed at the miracles that occur. When your will and the Higher will are aligned, all things become possible.

Affirmations

1. I am a channel for Higher wisdom.

2. Divine love uses me for its healing purposes.

3. I let go and let God.

4. I will Thy will.

5. I follow my intuition where it takes me.

6. *Your own* _____
   _____

Words to Consider
The decisive question for man is:
Is he related to something infinite or not?
That is the telling question of life.
Carl Jung

NINETEEN

Each Must Carry
His Own Burden

One of the great spiritual truths is that each person must work out his or her own personal salvation. When a person you care about is in trouble, you can reach out to support his or her healing, but past a certain point you can do no more. No matter how much you love, you cannot carry another person's burdens.

What can you do when someone you love is in pain? First, affirm that there is a purpose behind the experience. Know that the soul has some important lesson to learn that will be of great value to him or her.

Second, although you cannot directly intervene, your positive thoughts and prayers do make a difference. Visualize your friend surrounded by light and love. This type of healing acts directly on the soul level and does not encounter resistance from the conscious mind.

Finally, know that Divine protection is present. The forces of light are *always* available to the person who requests help. Ultimately, no soul can be lost; as all who ask will be guided to the safety of their spiritual home.

Affirmations

1. I take responsibility for my own life.

2. I allow others to take responsibility for their lives.

3. All things are working together for good in the lives of my loved ones.

4. I give others the freedom to discover and pursue their own paths.

5. I release the need to have others conform to my expectations.

6. *Your own* _____

_____

❧

_____   _____

Words to Consider
*Although all men share a common destiny, each individual
also has to work out his personal salvation for himself.
We can help each other find the meaning of life, but in the
last analysis, each is responsible for finding himself.*
Thomas Merton

TWENTY

Believe in Yourself

The Universe by nature is loving and supportive. Successful people know how to tap this support by enlisting the cooperation of others in order to achieve their goals. They also know that to receive support, they must first support themselves.

An entrepreneur once told his fellow inventors, "Before others will believe in you, you must believe in yourself. Your faith in yourself will attract investment capital more than any business plan could."

Unfortunately, the people who need the most support often have the hardest time asking for it. Growing up in an environment where love was denied, they don't believe they deserve it. This is why it is important to affirm our basic worthiness.

People want to extend themselves to you; it feels good to give. Encourage them to do so by believing in yourself and reaching out for what you want. The Universe will reach back to take your hand. Believe in yourself and others will believe in you. It cannot be otherwise.

Affirmations

1. I ask for what I want, and I receive it.

2. As my self-confidence grows, other people's confidence in me also expands.

3. I am worthy of success in all my endeavors.

4. The Universe supports me at all times and in all places.

5. I am attracting the people, finances, and circumstances to make my dreams come true.

6. *Your own* _____

_____

Words to Consider
Things do not change;
we change.
Henry David Thoreau

TWENTY-ONE

The Wounded Healer

Consider the following situations. A person born with a cleft palate becomes a surgeon specializing in the repair of cleft palates. A stutterer who corrects his problem becomes a speech therapist. A recovering alcoholic now works as a drug rehabilitation counselor. These individuals are living the story of the "wounded healer"—a person who uses the understanding gained in his own healing to assist others with the same problem.

A modern example of the wounded healer can be seen in the life of Bill W., the co-founder of Alcoholics Anonymous (AA). Faced with an illness over which he was powerless, Bill W. joined forces with Dr. Bob Smith to create a society of fellow sufferers. Since its inception in 1935, AA has become a source of healing and inspiration to millions of alcoholics around the world. The immensity of Bill W.'s suffering was redeemed by the infinite good that it accomplished.

Because we *all* suffer spiritual, emotional, mental, or physical "wounds," each of us has the capacity to be a wounded healer. Think back to times that you have been most effective in helping others. You will no doubt find that the wounds you helped to heal were the very same ones that you once overcame in yourself.

Thus, if you are dealing with a wound in your life right now, realize that one day your hurt will be a healing balm for another wounded soul. For this, give thanks.

Affirmations

1. I know that the wounds in my life have purpose and meaning.

2. Using the understanding and compassion gained from my own recovery, I reach out to others in the same situation.

3. I give thanks for my ability to be of service in this way.

4. My hurt can be a healing balm for the suffering of others.

5. I have discovered a hidden blessing in my situation.

6. *Your own* _____

_____

—————— ❧ ——————

Words to Consider
*In approaching the alcoholic, we have tried hard to capitalize on our
one great natural advantage. That is, of course, our personal
experience as drinkers who have recovered.*
Bill W., co-founder of Alcoholics Anonymous

Turning Lead into Gold

John Lennon once said, "Life is what happens to us when we are busy making other plans." As you follow the path of the inner voice with its fruits of peace and joy, you will also encounter your share of tests and challenges. While it is natural to ask, "Why me?" when adversity strikes, feeling victimized leaves you powerless to change the situation.

A better approach is to emulate the "triumphant survivors," those individuals who emerge from their ordeals strengthened and renewed. They understand the universal law that every adversity contains within it the seeds of an equivalent or greater good. The triumphant survivor says, "I would rather not have to deal with this challenge, but as long as I must, I will use it as an opportunity to grow and transform."

When adversity is faced in this way, miracles happen. The apparent curse becomes a divine blessing. Uninvited situations bring life-changing lessons. Here, then, is the alchemical secret—by using everything for our spiritual growth, we become victor instead of victim. By looking for the good in *all* things, we turn lead into gold.

Affirmations

1. I see all challenges as disguised opportunities.

2. God is working through each and every circumstance in my life.

3. I am a more loving and wise person because of what I have gone through.

4. When I can't change the situation, I change my attitude.

5. I give thanks for everything just the way it is.

6. *Your own* _____

_____

———————— ❦ ————————

Words to Consider
In the midst of winter
I found within me an invincible summer.
Albert Camus

TWENTY-THREE

Better the Pain Than to Remain the Same

The Barbara I met at my high school reunion was not the same person I had known a decade ago. A sensitive and caring person stood in the place of the driven and manipulative individual I remembered. Her soft gaze spoke of a new compassion and understanding. I asked a friend of Barbara's how this transformation occurred. "It's very simple," the friend replied. "She's been to hell and back."

Barbara's story is universal. It is the experience of pain—physical, emotional, or spiritual—that inspires us to start the search for something more. Many great teachers and healers began their spiritual quest as a way to cope with the pain of an illness, divorce, or similar loss. This discomfort forced them to abandon the status quo and take a new and uncharted course, a course that led to a major transformation.

Is pain the *only* way we can grow and transform? Not necessarily. As we work on ourselves and **learn** from our mistakes, the ups and downs of life become less intense. Lessons come in a more gentle manner. Once the heart is opened, it takes less effort to keep it that way.

You are moving to that point where joy and bliss are all-encompassing. Until then, your pain can be your greatest teacher.

Affirmations

1. I make my pain holy by finding meaning in it.

2. A broken heart is an open heart.

3. Because of my trials, I am a wiser and more compassionate person.

4. My pain has deepened me.

5. As I learn the lessons of my pain, my need for the pain decreases.

6. *Your own* _____

_____

❧

Words to Consider
People have a need to feel their pain.
Very often pain is the beginning of a great deal of awareness.
As an energy, it awakens consciousness.
Arnold Mindell

TWENTY-FOUR

Healing the Inner Child

The other day I passed by a homeless person sleeping in the street. I studied his face—rough, tired, defeated. As I experienced compassion for his situation, I went back in time and imagined what he looked like as an infant—full of hope and expectation. I also realized that despite outward circumstances, this inner child was still alive within him. For the next few days I perceived the inner child behind the masks of all whom I encountered.

What does this inner child want? It wants to be held, touched, and loved. It wants to belong. It wants to have fun, laugh, and play. What does this inner child provide? It gives us aliveness, energy, joy, and vitality. It gives us curiosity and a sense of wonder. It gives us life.

Most of us have paid too little attention to the child within. In a culture where striving for success makes life a "serious" business, we suffer from a common malady—a lack of connection with our childlike nature and the joy it brings.

It is said, "Unless you become as a little child, you cannot enter the kingdom of God." Resolve each day to ask your child what he or she needs or wants. Spend time getting to know him or her. Then note the increased vitality that comes from connecting with that central part of yourself.

Affirmations

1. I love my inner child.

2. I give my inner child the attention it asks for.

3. I now allow my inner child to participate in my daily affairs.

4. My life is filled with joy and vitality.

5. I create ample time for play.

6. *Your own* _____

——————— ❧ ———————

Words to Consider
The secret of genius is to carry the spirit of childhood into old age.
Bertrand Russell

TWENTY-FIVE

Open Your Heart Again

One of the most moving examples of the opening of a hardened heart is the story of Scrooge in Dickens' *A Christmas Carol*. At an early age, Scrooge concluded that the world was a hard and cruel place. Making the accumulation of money his primary goal, he closed himself off from his fellow human beings. Although he attained worldly riches, he was spiritually desolate.

Then, on Christmas Eve, he was graced with the opportunity to make a new choice—to open his heart to life. His physical wealth began to have a purpose. After his conversion, he paid for the operation that healed Tiny Tim and contributed to numerous charities throughout London.

I tell this story because there is a Scrooge in every one of us. In some area of life, you and I have hardened our hearts. Perhaps it is a former lover whom we have not forgiven; or we are angry at a political group that opposes our point of view; or an early wound has left a trail of hurt and cynicism.

Whatever the person or circumstance, the solution is the same—open your heart again. If the old pain comes to the surface, relax and breathe into the hurt. As your heart softens and expands, a deep compassion will fill your being. Like Scrooge, you are being reborn to a new life. You are being redeemed by the healing power of love.

Affirmations

1. I open myself to the power of love.

2. I allow the hard places in my heart to soften.

3. I release all past hurts and resentments.

4. I am willing to risk again.

5. The more vulnerable I become, the more love I can experience.

6. *Your own* _____

_____

——————— ❦ ———————

Words to Consider
*Do what you will with another person;
but never put them out of your heart.*
The Dalai Lama

TWENTY-SIX

Forgive and Move On

An essential aid to following the path of the inner voice is practicing forgiveness. Resentment comes from the Latin word *resentir*—to feel over and over again. By repeatedly re-experiencing the old resentments, we are less apt to hear our intuition, which exists only in the present.

When Jean married, she had not completed her unfinished business with her father. Consequently, she projected her old resentments onto her husband. Her desire to love him was distorted by the hurt and anger from the past. This is why it is said that until we complete our source relationships, we are never truly in another relationship.

Forgiving can also help you take back your power. As long as you believe that someone else's actions are the cause of your present difficulties, you are powerless to change. Letting go of blame allows you to take responsibility for your life.

All this adds up to a single point. Forgiveness is an act of self-kindness. It liberates your life force. It completes the past. Choose now to heal your old unfinished business. It is time to let go of the pain. Place your hurt on an altar and surrender it to God. Set yourself and others free.

Affirmations

1. I forgive and forget.

2. I am at peace with all that happens.

3. I release the old hurts.

4. I open my heart again.

5. I remember the past without the pain.

6. *Your own* _____
    _____

_____   _____

Words to Consider
The old law of "an eye for an eye"
leaves everybody blind.
Martin Luther King, Jr.

TWENTY-SEVEN

Letting Go

According to a Japanese legend, two monks were walking down the road when they saw a finely dressed young woman standing before a large mud puddle. She explained that she had no way of crossing the water without ruining her clothes. Without saying a word, the first monk picked her up in his arms and lifted her safely across the obstacle.

A few hours later the second monk said in an accusatory tone, "How could you have picked up that lady? Don't you know that the rules strictly forbid us to touch a member of the opposite sex?" His friend smiled and then replied, "I put the woman down back at the puddle. Are you still carrying her?"

Like the second monk, many of us are still carrying old hurts, resentments, and lost opportunities that we picked up many mud puddles ago. As long as we remain stuck in the past, we cannot fully hear the inner voice which speaks to us in the present. Thus, in order to tap our intuition, we need to release and heal our unfinished business.

By following the example of the first monk, we can put the past down and walk on. See your past experiences as teachings that have guided you to this present moment. An endless array of opportunities and possibilities lie before you. Immerse yourself in this good, and the old hurts will have no place left to make their home.

Affirmations

1. I release the pain of my disappointed expectations.

2. I let go of the old and make way for the new.

3. As I free myself from the past, my energy becomes available for the present.

4. The purpose and meaning of my past experiences are now revealed to me.

5. I make peace with my past.

6. *Your own* _____

_____

———————— ❦ ————————

Words to Consider
Always forgive your enemies—nothing annoys them so much.
Oscar Wilde

TWENTY-EIGHT

Moving through Loss

The nature of the material world is impermanence. Everything that begins in time will end in time. Nothing lasts forever. To this extent, we all experience loss.

But the pain of loss does not have to create long-term suffering. If we embrace the pain and feel our grief, a remarkable thing happens—the pain gradually recedes. This is what is meant by the saying, "The only way out of the pain is to embrace the pain." It is when we attempt to avoid the pain that suffering arises.

Another approach to loss is to appreciate the joy that you gained from that which is now gone—whether it is a person, an animal, or a phase of life that just ended. As a child who lost his cat remarked, "I miss my kitty. I'm glad I had him though. I'm glad he had the chance to live here and be my friend."

Finally, realize that the essence of a material form, which is love, never dies. In this sense, there is no such thing as loss. This is why Christ left his disciples with the words, "I am with you always, even unto the end of the world." In our lives as well, whatever we have loved can never leave us.

Affirmations

1. I allow myself to feel my feelings.

2. As I embrace my pain and sadness, I begin to feel better.

3. Although I grieve for what I lost, I know that a greater good will follow.

4. I am grateful that I have had the chance to love.

5. That which I love is always with me.

6. *Your own* _____
   _____

Words to Consider
There is no death; there is no separation.
There is only love.
A Course in Miracles

TWENTY-NINE

You Can't Heal What You Can't Feel

You are like a diamond that is continually being polished and perfected. As this purification proceeds, old thought forms and negative patterns rise to the surface to be released. Past unfinished business must be completed. Old traumas that have been stored in the body ask to be discharged.

This is not a bad thing—far from it. The fact that painful events are being re-experienced is a sign that healing is taking place. Although you may feel tempted to run from these feelings, let yourself experience them. As you allow yourself to feel the pain, the pain diminishes and eventually disappears.

Spirit is always helping you to release that which you no longer need. Let go of the resistance and surrender to the process. Complete the past and move on. Once you have done the work, you will never have to repeat it. How good it feels to be free!

Affirmations

1. I feel my feelings.

2. I move towards my feelings, knowing they are my friends.

3. Better the pain than to remain the same.

4. Experiencing the truth of my past liberates me from its influence.

5. I emerge from my ordeal healed and transformed.

6. *Your own* _____

   _____

———— ————

Words to Consider
The only way out is through.
The only way to heal the pain is to embrace the pain.
Fritz Perls

THIRTY

The Strength to Overcome

Life is a process of meeting and solving problems. Solving problems is a way that we test and develop our spiritual muscle. Think of outstanding people such as Abraham Lincoln, Mahatma Gandhi, and Helen Keller. Lincoln faced the problem of a divided country; Gandhi, an oppressed India; Keller, her personal handicaps. In rising to meet their challenges, these individuals expressed the qualities of vision, courage, fortitude, and compassion. They became great not in spite of, but **because of** their problems.

Problems often come to us in the form of crisis. The Chinese glyph for the word *crisis* contains two symbols: one means **danger** and the other **opportunity.** When an obstacle is before you, use it to create a beneficial result. As with Lincoln, Gandhi, and Keller, let your problems bring out your greatness.

Rather than pray for a life that is problem-free, ask for one that is solution-full. Instead of requesting that God remove the mountain before you, seek the strength to climb it. Remember that the best students always get the toughest problems. Love the problems you have, and their priceless gifts will be yours.

Affirmations

1. My problems strengthen and bring out the best in me.

2. I face my problems courageously.

3. I welcome new challenges into my life.

4. I uncover hidden blessings in difficult circumstances.

5. When a crisis arises, I acknowledge the danger but embrace the opportunity.

6. *Your own* _____
    _____

———— ❦ ————

Words to Consider
In life, the difficult periods are the best periods to gain experience and shore up determination. As a result, my mental status is much improved because of them.
The Dalai Lama

THIRTY-ONE

The Future Is Not What It Used to Be

With the pace of change continuing to accelerate, the future is not what it used to be. From one moment to the next, no one can be certain of anything. Your job, your marriage, your relationship to your children—none of these may be the same next year, next month, or even next week.

How does one survive this changing landscape? First, by being flexible and adaptable—ready to change course at any moment. Be prepared to "roll with the punches" and release your old attachments or current expectations.

Second, practice living one day at a time. Realize that the only thing that you can really affect is how you feel this instant. By focusing on the present moment, you can continue to experience peace and joy—no matter how the outer circumstances may change.

Finally, know that the removal of old securities opens the way to new opportunities. Human consciousness is moving to ever higher levels of awareness. How much easier the journey is when we flow with the process of change.

Affirmations

1. I welcome *all* change into my life.

2. I am able to adapt to any situation that I encounter.

3. I am given just what I need for the optimal learning experience.

4. No matter what life deals me, I always have a winning hand.

5. Spirit guides and directs my path each step along the way.

6. *Your own* _____

_____

—————— ❦ ——————

Words to Consider
I don't believe in predicting, especially about the future.
Casey Stengel

THIRTY-TWO

Who Is Directing This Movie?

Most of us would like to believe that we are the person best qualified to direct our life's movie. But when we attempt to run things solely from the perspective of the ego, we soon discover the limits of its power. Despite our best intentions, chaos and confusion abound on the set. Life lacks a quality of flow, joy, and peace.

"How can this be?" you may ask. "In order to run my life, I must be in charge. I must be in control. What other way is there?"

There is an alternative. Let the real director run the show. From now on, take your cues from that universal Intelligence which dwells within you. If you are told to appear in a scene where you don't think you belong, have faith. Watch as people and resources appear at the right time and place, and all unfolds in Divine order.

Make the choice to turn your life over to your higher director. Instead of trying to control everything, trust that the Universe will handle the details. Letting go may be scary at first. But if you follow this path, your life will work out more beautifully than you ever could have imagined.

Affirmations

1. I let go and let God.

2. I let the Universe handle the details.

3. When I release the need to be in control, everything works out.

4. I trust my intuition to show me the way.

5. My life unfolds in Divine order.

6. *Your own* _____

   _____

———————————— ❦ ————————————

Words to Consider
Human conduct is ever unreliable until it is anchored in the Divine.
Sri Yukteswar

THIRTY-THREE

Hang On Tightly, Let Go Lightly

In ancient Japan, there once lived a solitary monk in a monastery high atop a mountain. One day a woman in the town below became pregnant by a local fisherman. Wanting to protect her friend, she accused the monk of the deed. Following the baby's birth, the villagers took him to the monk and said, "Here! It was you who did this. You must now become responsible for the child." After a short pause, the monk simply bowed his head and said, "Ah, so."

Although he had been used to living alone, the monk soon developed a fondness for his new companion and became a good parent to him. One day the boy's mother became gravely ill. As she lay dying, she confessed to the wrong she had done. Once more, the townspeople took the long walk up the mountain and spoke to the monk. "A mistake has been made. You are not the real father of the child. Although you have dutifully cared for him all these years, now you must give him up." After a moment of reflection the monk bowed and replied, "Ah, so."

Our lives are constantly changing. People and things come and go. All situations that we create are only temporary. By viewing life from this larger perspective, our monastic friend was able to face both loss and gain with peace and tranquility.

It is not always easy to be detached, especially when we must release a situation or a person we love. But the new always rises to replace the old. And sooner or later you will arrive at that point where you, too, can smile and serenely say, "Ah, so."

Affirmations

1. I am serene, calm, and peaceful in the midst of change.

2. I accept the up times and the down times as having equal value in my life.

3. I see Divine perfection and order in all things.

4. I release those parts of my life that I need to let go.

5. From a peaceful place in the center of my being, I witness my life unfolding.

6. *Your own* _____

_____

Words to Consider
One to me is loss and gain,
One to me is pleasure and pain,
One to me is fame and shame.
Proverb

THIRTY-FOUR

The Universe Knows Best

How many times have you wanted something very badly, only to realize at a later date that having it would have been a major disaster? Often we pursue a certain want or desire when the Universe has something entirely different planned—something which is for our higher good.

For years, Ann wanted to run her own day-care center. An opportunity arose for her to buy a local business, but the deal fell through at the last minute. Bitterly disappointed, she could not understand why her heart's desire was denied her. Then one day, she and her husband found out about a business that was for sale in a city where they had always wanted to live. Within weeks, they bought the business and moved to their new location. Ann gave thanks that the first opportunity did *not* work out.

From our earthly vantage point, we can't always see the big picture. We are like mice running in an open field, sensing what is in front of our noses. Only from the perspective of the eagle can the entire landscape be viewed.

Fortunately, there is a part of yourself that can see like the eagle. You can turn over your life and your plans to that higher vision, and then say with assurance, "It's all God's work. It's all in God's hands. And I am at peace with this."

Affirmations

1. I let the Higher will express itself in all my affairs.

2. The Universe knows best.

3. Higher wisdom illumines and directs my path.

4. All things are working together for good in my life.

5. I let go of my attachment to final results.

6. *Your own* _____

   _____

———————— ❧ ————————

Words to Consider
WILL POWER—
Our willingness to be used by a Higher Power.
Alcoholics Anonymous

THIRTY-FIVE

God Does Great Things through Me

When the renowned composer Johann Sebastian Bach was praised for his music, he responded, "To God goes the glory." When a well-known writer was asked to reveal his secret, he said, "I am simply the person whom the words came through." Like many who have excelled in their field, these artists knew that it is God who makes us great, that it is the spirit within that expresses its perfect purpose through us.

God wants to do great things through you, too. In your prayers and meditation, ask that Infinite Intelligence work through you for the highest good of yourself and others. Ask to be a channel for the expression of the Divine plan. Then trust that spirit will guide you each step of the way, ensuring the right outcome of every situation and providing for all your needs.

You have a purpose and a mission—something to contribute during your stay on earth. Even now spirit is beckoning you to fulfill your unique greatness. Listen and you will hear the call.

Affirmations

1. God is doing great things through me.

2. I am a channel for Divine inspiration.

3. Each day creative ideas are revealed to me.

4. I listen to and follow my inner voice.

5. I am in a partnership with the Infinite that leads to success.

6. Your own _____

_____

———————— ❧ ————————

Words to Consider
Place yourself in the middle of the stream of power and wisdom which flows through your life. Then, without effort, you are impelled to truth and to perfect contentment.
Ralph Waldo Emerson

THIRTY-SIX

Keep the Faith

When following the inner voice, one must deal with the experience of uncertainty. The future is not laid out and neatly planned. There are no guarantees. In the end, it all comes down to trust—trusting that the support will be there; that the money will come; that if one path does not work out, another one will open up.

We can develop this trust from experience. We step out in faith the first time, and the Universe supports us. We step out again and the assistance is there. After several experiences, we begin to feel comfortable living by faith—our "invisible means of support." We no longer need to know ahead of time how everything will work out.

So make the decision. Let go of the worry, the anxiety, and the doubt. Have faith in your connection to universal principles, for it is here that your true security lies. The Universe will not abandon you if you maintain your connection to it. Keep the faith, and the faith will keep you.

Affirmations

1. I am led by my Higher Power.

2. I trust my intuition to guide and direct my way.

3. My will and the Divine will are one.

4. I release my need to worry and doubt.

5. Every day my faith is growing stronger.

6. *Your own* _____

   _____

———————— ❦ ————————

Words to Consider
*The only limits to our realization of tomorrow will be
our doubts of today.
Let us move forward with a strong and active faith.*
Franklin D. Roosevelt

THIRTY-SEVEN

The Eleventh Hour

Recently I witnessed the birth of my friend's third child. Because of the infant's large size, labor proved more difficult than expected. After eight hours of strenuous contractions, in pain and totally exhausted, the mother resigned herself to a Caesarean section.

Then a gentle and sympathetic doctor arrived. He suggested that we elevate the mother's legs and slightly rotate the hips. With these subtle changes, the momentum shifted. The birth process accelerated. Beginning with the head and then the shoulders, a healthy baby Patrick sprang from the womb.

The experience can only be described as miraculous. At the moment everyone gave up, grace descended. A force outside of ourselves intervened and "in the twinkling of an eye" the situation changed. Before we knew it, the birth had occurred.

The next time you are stuck and feel like there is no way out, think of baby Patrick. Like him, you may be just moments away from a glorious new life. Soon, you will be pushed through the birth canal into the light of day.

Affirmations

1. I am in the process of being reborn.

2. I can sense the light at the end of the tunnel.

3. Just when all seems lost, help arrives.

4. I call on the Universe and am lifted to safety.

5. I am never given more than God and I can handle.

6. *Your own* _____

   _____

——————— ❧ ———————

Words to Consider
Enlightenment begins on the other side of despair.
Jean-Paul Sartre

THIRTY-EIGHT

One Step at a Time

An important key to progress on the path is to take it one step at a time. Just as investing a little on a regular basis builds long-term wealth, the little gains we make each day pay off in spiritual dividends. As a successful musical group explained, "We spent years preparing for our overnight success."

Taking it one step at a time means living in the present moment, letting life gradually reveal itself to us. Some people get nervous and want to know the final outcome. But how can we know an outcome that hasn't yet occurred?! Trust in the process, and the perfect result will occur.

When our faith wavers, we often get ahead of ourselves and try to figure out what is going to happen. This "future tripping" removes us from our source of guidance in the present. Sometimes we try to hit it big in a hurry. But there is no fooling the Universe. Sooner or later we will have to go back and retrace the steps that we skipped. The only place where *success* comes before *work* is in the dictionary.

Whatever the goal or desire, approach it one step at a time. Small measures consistently taken guarantee progress. Eventually you will emerge victorious, having attained a reward that you have truly earned.

Affirmations

1. I patiently work towards my good.

2. Each new step is revealed to me precisely when I need it.

3. By living in the present, I create a wonderful future.

4. I trust in my guidance.

5. My life is unfolding perfectly.

6. *Your own* _____

    _____

———————— 🍎 ————————

Words to Consider
Mile by mile, life's a trial.
Yard by yard, it's not so hard.
Inch by inch, it's a cinch.
Proverb

THIRTY-NINE

Turning It Over

There comes a time in facing a challenge when we have done all that we can, and still the situation remains unresolved. This is the time to turn the problem over and release our cares into the hands of spirit. When we let the Universe take charge, anything becomes possible. God can do for us what we could not do for ourselves.

If you find that you have reached such an impasse, try the following: in your mind's eye place the problem upon an imaginary altar. Then say, "I turn this over to you, spirit. From now on, you are in charge." As you walk away from the altar, feel the inner peace which comes from knowing that all is in Divine hands.

Despairing of ever getting published, a young writer used this approach. He placed his manuscript on his inner altar and moved on to another project. Two weeks later, the book was accepted by a major publisher for a substantial advance. Turning to his agent he said, "I want to thank whoever is responsible, because it certainly wasn't me."

It is good to realize that we do not have to do everything alone. Help is available. Invisible hands come to support us at the right time. As the psalmist assures us, "Cast thy burden upon the Lord, and He shall sustain thee."

Affirmations

1. When I have done all I can, I turn over the outcome to God.

2. I release my attachment to the results.

3. I step out of the way and let spirit do its work.

4. Spirit is doing for me what I cannot do for myself.

5. I attract perfect support when I need it.

6. *Your own* _____

_____

—————— ❧ ——————

Words to Consider
Do your best and leave to God the rest.
Proverb

FORTY

The Readiness Is All

As we follow the path of the inner voice, timing plays a critical role. We draw to ourselves the experiences we need, when we need them. As each phase is mastered, the next appears.

It is when we try to force or rush things that trouble arises. Children who are pushed to achieve too early in life burn out at a young age. Receiving something before you are ready for it can be worse than not getting it at all. This is why a wise person once said, "I pray not for enlightenment, but simply to be ready when it comes."

Sometimes we think that we are ready for some good when in fact we are not. The delays we suffer often indicate that more time and preparation are needed. Several years ago, a friend wrote a screenplay that she was sure was ready to be made into a movie. At the time, no one was interested. Five years later, she became inspired to rewrite the script and alter the plot. A studio immediately made an offer.

If you are facing delays in your plans, remember the saying, "With every delay, there's a blessing on its way." Be patient and do what is required. When the time is right, the result you are seeking will manifest itself with ease. And because you are ready for it, it will be ready for you.

Affirmations

1. My life unfolds in perfect Divine order.

2. As I open myself to success, success opens to me.

3. Whatever I am ready for is ready for me.

4. I am ready for prosperity and abundance to flow into my life.

5. I live according to the Universe's time schedule.

6. *Your own* _____

_____

———————— ❦ ————————

Words to Consider
With every delay, there's a blessing on its way.
Proverb

107

FORTY-ONE

If God Seems Far Away, Who Moved?

At the center of our being a fullness of life exists that wants to flow through us as vitality, love, harmony, happiness, and success. Why, then, are we not more in touch with it?

Consider the following image. You are standing outside on a bright, cloudless day complaining that you cannot see the sun, when you notice that you have been standing under an umbrella. If as little a thing as an umbrella can block out the magnificence of the sun, how easy it is for our fears, doubts, and feelings of unworthiness to block the connection to our source. But just as the sun continues to shine even behind the appearance of clouds, our inner knowing is ready to communicate with us in the midst of our despair.

How do we reopen the channels and allow the flow to reenter our lives? First, we must truly desire to communicate with our center and set aside a time each day to do so. Then, get quiet and begin to **listen**. Soon you will hear that still small voice within.

Your divine self is patiently waiting for you to acknowledge it. It quietly but persistently knocks on the door of your consciousness. Open that door and a presence of love and joy will fill your being.

Affirmations

1. I hear the knock of truth upon the door of my conscious-
    ness, and I rush to respond.

2. God's presence enters to fill my soul, and I experience a
    deep and joyous peace.

3. From a place deep within me, I feel content.

4. Each day, I am more in touch with my intuition.

5. I am continually nourished by a fountain of love that
    springs forth from my center.

6. *Your own* _____

    _____

———————— ❧ ————————

Words to Consider
The winds of grace are blowing all the time.
You have only to raise your sail.
Sri Ramakrishna

FORTY-TWO

The Wisdom of Insecurity

Life is dynamic and ever changing. There are no guarantees. The "security" that so many search for does not exist; the best that we can hope for is "temporary stability."

In searching for that elusive security, it is easy to fall into a rut and feel trapped by circumstances. But circumstances can control us only when we give them the power to do so. Every day we read stories of individuals who have decided to break out of the mold and to do something outrageous.

Accepting the wisdom of insecurity is liberating. Knowing that nothing is certain reminds us to keep life fluid and to live one day at a time. When my best friend and I traveled around the country, not knowing where we would be from week to week, life became an ongoing adventure. Although we had nothing, we possessed everything.

Are there any places in your life where you feel trapped or stuck? Remember that nothing can trap you unless you let it. It is never too late for change.

Affirmations

1. My true security rests in my connection to my Higher Power.

2. I live a day at a time and let the future take care of itself.

3. I am open to change at any moment.

4. My life is full of possibilities.

5. I have faith in myself and in God to cope with any situation that arises.

6. *Your own* _____

   _____

_____ _____

Words to Consider
Life is a series of natural and spontaneous changes.
Let things flow naturally forward in whatever way they like.
Lao Tsu

FORTY-THREE

A Satisfied Mind

A wise physician once said, "If you lose your health, you've lost a great deal; but if you lose your peace of mind, you've lost everything!" A positive state of mind is a truly precious asset.

We live in a world that places a premium on doing. Our happiness is measured by the size of our bank account or a list of our accomplishments. But all of our doing cannot substitute for a peaceful state of **being**—what the gospel singer calls "a satisfied mind."

This idea is illustrated in the biblical story of Mary and Martha. While Martha was rushing about trying to manipulate the world of effects, Mary turned within and raised her state of consciousness. Jesus commented, "Martha, Martha, you are worried and troubled by many things. But one thing is needed. Mary has chosen the better part which will not be taken from her."

By making a satisfied mind her first priority, Mary had chosen wisely. You, too, can rise above the strife and confusion of the external world and experience the "peace of God, which passeth all understanding." In carrying this peace into your outer activities, you will become a far more powerful and effective force for change.

Affirmations

1. I value and nurture my inner life.

2. I go within and tap the experiences of love, peace, and joy.

3. I am serene and content.

4. I give myself time to be.

5. I enjoy relaxing and being at rest.

6. *Your own* _____

_____

——————————— ❦ ———————————

Words to Consider
Happiness resides not in possessions or in gold;
The feeling of happiness dwells in the soul.
Democritus

FORTY-FOUR

Let Peace Begin with Me

For the dream of world peace to become a reality, the most important link in the process must be the individual. Because the individual mind is connected to the collective or group mind, each person's peacefulness elevates the group consciousness. This truth is expressed in the lyrics from a popular song, "Let there be peace on earth and let it begin with me."

The greatest obstacle to peace is fear. Fear arises from the experience of *separation*. Love, which joins and unifies all things, is the antidote to fear. Our task, then, is to release old thoughts of fear and separation and replace them with thoughts of love and unity. This shift occurs moment by moment, as we learn to choose peace over conflict.

One person committed to peacefulness is a powerful force in the universe. When a small but significant number of people engage in this process, all of humanity will feel the change. You have your part to play in shifting the balance that will usher in a glorious new era.

Let there be peace on earth and let it begin with you.

Affirmations

1. Peace of mind is my primary goal.

2. I let go of fear and experience inner peace.

3. In all of my affairs, I choose peace over conflict.

4. I would rather be happy than be right.

5. The world in which I live is a place of peace.

6. *Your own* _____

_____

——————— ———————

Words to Consider
Imagine all the people living life in peace.
John Lennon

FORTY-FIVE

Joy Is My Compass

Today and always, let joy be your compass. When choosing a direction in life, choose the path of your heart. Do what you love. Follow your bliss.

Fun is an underestimated emotion in our culture. We are told as children, "If you waste time having fun, you won't get anything serious accomplished." Yet most successful people describe their work as being incredibly joyful. An office that sings with laughter is always more productive. As one executive remarked, "The more I enjoy my work, the more efficient I become."

Joy and laughter improve the quality of our relationships. Couples who lighten up rarely split up. Laughing at a difficult situation fosters detachment and understanding. It is only when we get too serious that trouble arises.

Since love is the highest expression of the Divine, following the path of love and joy will lead you to God-consciousness. What more is there?

Affirmations

1. Today and forever, joy is my compass.

2. I choose that which brings me and others joy.

3. As I lighten up, I draw closer to enlightenment.

4. I follow the path of my heart.

5. I play for pay.

6. *Your own* _____

_____

——————— ❦ ———————

Words to Consider
I certainly am a happy person.
How could one know God and not be joyous?
Peace Pilgrim

FORTY-SIX

Amazing Grace

For those who walk the path of the inner voice, grace is the ultimate blessing. Not only are we guided by grace, but it is grace that has enabled us to take the first step on this wondrous journey.

Think of the times when you were lifted out of disaster at the eleventh hour. Recall those turning points when unseen forces intervened in your life. The right job turned up when you needed it. Through a series of seeming coincidences, you were led to a person who provided the help you were seeking. An unexpected source of money arrived to pay the bills.

As a cloud-covered sky can block out the rays of the sun, so our doubts and fear can block the perception of God's grace. Still, the sun is always shining, even when we can't see it. The help is still there, even when we don't realize it. And in the midst of our unbelief, grace still enters our lives.

We are not alone. We may call it a guardian angel or unexplained good fortune, but there is a benevolent force at work in our lives, guiding us each step along the way. More than anything else, the experience of grace gives us the courage to continue listening to the inner voice. For the love that has guided you to this point would not have done so unless it was prepared to lead you on—to the fulfillment of your highest and truest calling.

Affirmations

1. I give thanks for the good that has graced my life.

2. I am truly blessed.

3. I appreciate all the help I receive.

4. My life overflows with abundance and prosperity.

5. The light of God surrounds me.

6. *Your own* _____

_____

—————— ❧ ——————

Words to Consider
*Through many dangers, toils and snares I have already come.
Tis grace that hath brought me safe thus far and grace
will lead me home.*
John Newton

FORTY-SEVEN

Oneness

A fundamental principle of the universe is that of oneness. A basic unity connects all of creation. On a cellular level, the DNA of all living organisms is virtually identical. Despite appearances, we are more similar than different.

Why, then, does conflict and fighting persist within the human family? Because the ego, the separate self, maintains the illusion of separateness. We mistakenly believe that our interests are different from our neighbor's and act to oppose the so-called enemy.

The changing nature of the world is forcing us to change our thinking. We live in a global economy and environment where all fates are interconnected. When rain forests are cut down in the Amazon, the climate is warmed in New York. What happens to my neighbor directly impacts my life.

Take time to meditate on the oneness of humankind. See yourself as a citizen of planet Earth as well as a member of the human community, not bound to any group or nation. We are one body. As each of us makes this shift in consciousness, ripples will spread through the group mind until we recognize the truth expressed by the comic strip character Pogo: "We has met the enemy, and he is us."

Affirmations

1. I am joined in consciousness with my brothers and sisters around the planet.

2. I am more like others than I am different.

3. I forgive those who I perceive have wronged me.

4. I make peace with my so-called enemies.

5. I am connected to all beings.

6. Your own _____
   _____

_____ ❦ _____

Words to Consider
Man did not weave the web of life, he is merely a strand in it.
What he does to the web he does to himself.
Chief Seatlh
(after whom Seattle was named)

FORTY-EIGHT

Acceptance

One of life's paradoxes is that in order to change an unwanted situation, we must first accept it the way it is. If you wish to move forward in your life, first make peace with what you are presently experiencing.

John was working at a job that he had ceased to enjoy and could not wait to leave. Yet despite his extensive job search, he was unable to find new employment. Realizing that you can't leave a situation without spiritual injury unless you leave it lovingly, John decided to make peace with his job and to bless the people in it. This change of attitude freed him to move on to new employment.

Accepting people as they are is also transformational. For years, a man tried to get his elderly mother to stop complaining. One day he gave up trying to change her and accepted her faults. This experience of unconditional love opened her heart to the point where she stopped condemning herself and others.

If there is some area of your life that you are seeking to change, first practice acceptance. By acknowledging where you are and giving thanks for the good that you have received, you will release an energy that will transform you and your present circumstances.

Affirmations

1. I bless and accept where I am.

2. I love and support myself and others just the way we are.

3. I forgive myself for being imperfect.

4. I see the purpose and meaning of my present circumstances.

5. I am at peace with myself and the world.

6. *Your own* _____

   _____

   _____ ❧ _____

Words to Consider
God grant me the serenity to accept the things I cannot change,
the courage to change the things I can,
and the wisdom to know the difference.
The Serenity Prayer

FORTY-NINE

Do It from Love

In determining the quality of your life, there is an important question to ask: "How much love do I express?"

How much love do I express in my *work*? Do I love my work or is my job just a job? Do I enjoy the people I work with?

How much love do I express in my *relationships*? What level of intimacy do I experience with my significant other, children, friends, and relatives?

How much love do I express in my *finances*? Am I holding on to money out of fear? Or am I using it to empower and support others, both in my investments and through giving?

How much love do I express in my *health*? Do I love and nurture my body and supply it with proper nutrition, exercise, and rest?

How much love do I express in my *spiritual life*? Do I worship a loving God or do I fear a God of wrath and punishment?

By taking inventory of these areas, you will arrive at a simple conclusion—that how good you feel is a function of the amount of love in your life. If you wish to feel better at the deepest level of your being, the solution is clear. Love more.

Affirmations

1. The primary motivating force in my life is love.

2. Whatever I do, I do from love.

3. Each day, I follow my bliss.

4. I am willing to take the risk of being close.

5. I walk through life with an open heart.

6. *Your own* _____

_____

_____ ❦ _____

Words to Consider
It is only with the heart that one can see rightly.
What is essential is invisible to the eye.
Antoine de Saint-Exupery

FIFTY

Look for the Good

Life is an interpretive experience. What happens is less important than how we respond to our circumstances. An intense stimulus that some people report as pain, others report as pleasure. It is we who decide what the interpretation will be.

Are you a "goodfinder"? A recent study of the country's millionaires showed that the most common trait they all shared was the ability to discover good in any situation. This trait is also common in "triumphant survivors"—those individuals who overcome adversity and emerge strengthened and renewed.

A sincere spiritual seeker suffering from a chronic illness wondered, "Why haven't my prayers been answered?" One day, in deep meditation the reply came: "Look for the good in your situation and you will see that the answer has already been provided." Suddenly this woman realized that her crisis provided a wonderful opportunity. She embarked on a program of nutrition, exercise, and yoga which led to a dramatic improvement in the quality of her life.

Abraham Lincoln once said, "Most people are about as happy as they make up their minds to be." Your state of mind is up to you. Choose now to look for the good.

Affirmations

1. I look for the good in all my affairs.

2. No matter what the circumstances, I find something positive that I can learn from them.

3. I experience *all* events as enhancing my spiritual growth.

4. For every loss, there exists a corresponding gain.

5. What goes down must come up.

6. *Your own* _____
   _____

_____ ❦ _____

Words to Consider
Nothing is good or bad but thinking makes it so.
Shakespeare

FIFTY-ONE

The Power of Optimism

A truly powerful force in the universe is that of optimism. Optimism lies at the root of our mental and physical health. Feelings of hope can stimulate the body's immune system and inspire recovery from a critical illness.

Optimism expresses itself in the persistence and resilience of living things. A child learning to walk repeatedly falls down and picks himself up until he stands erect. A decade after the eruption of Mt. St. Helens destroyed the local ecology, life has reestablished itself on this volcano with amazing abundance and rapidity. And despite its hostile environment, a sole dandelion miraculously pushes itself up through a crack in the concrete. That dandelion is optimistic that it can and will survive.

In the long run, the forces of love and life **always** triumph over those of fear and death. No matter how challenging the obstacles or difficult the tests, there is always cause for optimism.

Affirmations

1. I have faith that all things are working together for good in my life.

2. I expect the best, and I get it.

3. I see my glass as half full rather than as half empty.

4. When I fall down, I pick myself up and try again.

5. I am empowered by my optimism.

6. *Your own* _____
   _____

—————— ❦ ——————

Words to Consider
The natural flights of the human mind are not from pleasure to pleasure, but from hope to hope.
Samuel Johnson

FIFTY-TWO

The Truth Shall Make You Free

Listening to the inner voice means living a life of honesty and integrity. As Gandhi stated, "For me, God and *truth* are convertible terms. Devotion to the truth is the sole reason for my existence."

The truth is inescapable. There once was a wise teacher who gave each of two men a chicken and told them to kill the chickens where no one would see. The first man went behind the barn and killed his chicken. The second returned after three days with a live chicken. "Why didn't you kill the chicken?" the teacher asked. The man replied, "You told me to go where no one was looking, but everywhere I go, the chicken sees." It is the same in our lives. We can deceive others and even our conscious mind, but everywhere we go our own God-self sees.

Telling the truth to ourselves and others is liberating. Once you acknowledge the truth of a dysfunctional relationship, you can do something about it. Once you admit that you are powerless over an addiction, you can begin to treat it. If, however, you deny the problem, there is no way to change it. This is the meaning of the saying, "You are only as sick as your secrets."

The great historian Cicero said, "Our minds possess by nature an insatiable desire to know the truth." Let us live, breathe, and speak this truth so that we may come to know the beauty and perfection of our inner divinity.

Affirmations

1. I am honest with myself and with others.

2. I see the truth of what is.

3. I am willing to face the truth, even if it hurts.

4. The truth liberates and sets me free.

5. I release my old illusions and misperceptions.

6. *Your own* _____

_____

❦

Words to Consider
If you continue in my word, then you are my disciples indeed.
And you shall know the truth, and the truth shall make you free.
John 8:32

Reflections on Following Your Bliss

Never be afraid to tread the path alone.
Know which is your path and follow it wherever it may lead you.
Eileen Caddy

We are all on a journey—a journey of self-knowl-edge and self-discovery. The journey is a movement towards the highest that is within us.

Following the path of the inner voice is not easy. It takes courage, faith, and commitment. The false voices from within and without will urge you to abandon your heart's desire. But ultimately, being true to yourself is the only way to experience a life of joy and abundance.

Over the years, I have learned a number of lessons about following one's bliss which I would like to share with you:

- To hear the still small voice, **you must become quiet.** There are so many distractions clamoring for your attention. Choose the silence over the outer diversions.

- Faith requires living on **invisible means of support.** The support will always be there, even if you can't see it at first. Trust in the process and let the Universe handle the details.

- The key is not only trusting the Universe, but also **trusting yourself.** Believe that what you are doing is valid and that you can successfully meet any challenge that comes your way.

- **Commitment and perseverance** are essential in order to move through delays and disappointments. Our greatest glory lies not in never falling, but in *rising* every time we fall.

- Realize that **the Universe is the senior partner** and you are the junior partner. Let it take the lead. In the long run, everything that is not of God will come to naught.

- Learn to be **flexible and adaptable.** Change can happen in the twinkling of an eye. Be prepared to alter your plans at any moment.

- Now and always, **let your heart be your guide.** Let that which you love be the infallible touchstone that points the way home. As Pascal said, "The heart has its own reasons, which reason cannot understand."

The words of St. Theresa of Avila, written four centuries ago, beautifully summarize the loving support available to each of us when we choose to listen to and follow our inner voice.

Let nothing disturb thee,
Nothing afright thee;
All things are passing,
God never changes.

Patient endurance
Attaineth to all things.
Who God possesses
In nothing is wanting,
Alone God suffices.

Appendix A
How to Create a Healing Affirmation

An *affirmation* is a positive thought or idea that you consciously focus on in order to produce a desired result. The affirmation is a simple yet powerful tool that can heal and transform your most deeply held, limiting beliefs.

Creating affirmations to heal your life is a straightforward and enjoyable experience. The following seven-step procedure can be used to construct an affirmation for any area of your life. A more expanded version of this process can be found in the book *Words That Heal: Affirmations and Meditations for Daily Living,* by Douglas Bloch (Bantam Books).

1. **Pick an area of your life that you wish to work on.**
   The topic of the affirmation can involve a relationship, health, work, finances, peace of mind, etc.

2. **Decide what you want to occur in that area of life.**
   Ask yourself, "What would it feel like if this part of my life were healed? What is the end result I am seeking?"

3. **Using the *first person,* formulate a concise statement that expresses the desired outcome.**
   a) State or compose the affirmation in the **present** tense. Imagine the experience happening in *this* moment.
   b) State it **positively**. State what you *do* want, not what you don't want.

4. **Experience how the affirmation *feels*.**
   If the affirmation is going to work, it will feel right inside (ful*feel*ment brings ful*fill*ment).

5. **Repeat the affirmation.**
   Say it to yourself, say it out loud, and write it down. You might even want to make a cassette tape. Repetition is the mother of learning. When an affirmation is repeated, its message is impressed on the mind, thereby transforming previously held beliefs.

6. **Be consistent.**
   It is essential to use your affirmation on a daily basis in order to benefit from the principle of spaced repetition. In addition to the repetitions that spontaneously occur during the day, you may wish to set aside a specific time to focus on your affirmation.

7. **Turn over the final outcome to a Higher Power.**
   Sometimes your ego does not know what is in your best interest. The Universe **always** knows what is for your highest good. To align your affirmation with the will of your Higher self, you can use a prayer or invocation such as, "This or something better now manifests for me in totally satisfying and harmonious ways for the highest good of all concerned."

   Then, release your request into the hands of that loving Presence.

Appendix B
Healing Codependency through Affirmations

*A codependent person is one who at the moment of death
sees **another** person's life flashing before him.*

One reason that so many people do not follow their
inner voices is that they are busy following someone else's.
This tendency to live for other people instead of for oneself
has been called "codependency."

The use of affirmations is particularly beneficial for
codependent people. Codependency by definition implies a
focusing on people and things *outside* oneself. An affirmation, on the other hand, is something that comes from within. It is self-generated. Thus, by its very nature the affirmation guides the codependent person to discover his or her
own source of wisdom and knowing.

Moreover, the process of applying affirmations is
self-directed. The process by which affirmations are written
or created is a solitary one. Other people are not required.
Thus, the codependent individual does not run the risk of
becoming dependent on an authority figure or external guru.

Finally, because creating an affirmation involves
going within and tapping one's inner knowing, affirmations
provide a wonderful way for codependent people to learn to
trust themselves and their feelings.

The Master Affirmation for Codependency

Although various affirmations can be used successfully to transform specific beliefs held by codependent individuals, one "master affirmation" addresses a basic belief that underlies all the others: **"My primary responsibility is to myself."**

By absorbing the truth of this master affirmation, the codependent person can learn to love and nurture himself or herself, and thus break the cycle of seeking that nurturance through caring for others. When we establish *constructive* relationships with *ourselves*, our *destructive* relationships with *others* disappear.

It is helpful to remember that this affirmation needs to be balanced by an understanding of the give-and-take nature of relationships. Taking care of yourself does not mean cutting yourself off from other people. You become responsible **for** yourself in order that you can become responsible **to** others. When your cup is full and overflowing, then you can share and give of yourself.

General Affirmations for Codependency

The master affirmation for codependency was derived by responding to a prevalent belief exhibited by the codependent: "Other people come first. I come second." Other negative beliefs of codependent individuals can also be healed through affirmations. For every negative statement, a corresponding affirmation corrects the misperception and leads one towards independence and self-sufficiency.

When you catch yourself engaged in negative self-talk, say out loud, "Cancel! Cancel!" This phrase short-circuits the negative message. Next, replace the thought with an appropriate affirmation. Below are listed some examples showing how this process can be applied to negative statements commonly found in the self-talk of codependents.

Codependent Self-Talk	Therapeutic Affirmation
Other people control my life.	*I am responsible for my life.*
Others come first. I come second.	*I take care of myself and put my needs first.*
It's not right to be selfish.	*Loving myself supports me to love others.*
Others need me too much.	*My first responsibility is to myself.*

I am ashamed of who I am.	*I love and accept myself unconditionally.*
I can't do it.	*I am capable and competent.*
I need to be in control.	*I let go and let God.*
I don't trust myself.	*I acknowledge and follow my intuition.*
I don't deserve to have fun.	*I deserve to feel good.*
I don't deserve to be happy.	*I am worthy of joy.*
I don't trust life.	*I live in a loving universe.*
I'm afraid of intimacy.	*It is safe for me to open up.*
I always get trapped in relationships.	*I have the power to leave when I want to.*
I am always hurt in relationships.	*My relationships can be supportive and healing.*
I let others walk over me.	*I create strong boundaries.*
My anger is bad.	*My anger serves to protect me.*
I'm afraid to get angry.	*It's okay to feel my feelings.*

The beauty of this technique is that it can be used to transmute **any** negative codependent self-statement. Take any negative or limiting phrase that you say to yourself, write it down, and *rewrite* it as a healing affirmation. Use the following sentence as a guide.

I now release the statement that _____
_____ (write your old self-talk)
and replace it with _____
_____ (write your new self-talk or affirmation).

Using the Affirmation-Dialogue Process for Codependent Self-Talk

Once you have created your healing affirmation, you can work with it using the *affirmation-dialogue process* that we described at the beginning of the book. Here is how it worked for Andrea, who wrote the affirmation, "I take care of myself and meet my needs."

Affirmation	First Response	Second Response
I take care of myself and meet my needs.	How can I?	By asking for what I want.
I take care of myself and meet my needs.	John needs me too much.	He can learn to support himself.

143

I take care of myself and meet my needs.	I'm not worthy.	I am capable and competent.
I take care of myself and meet my needs.	I don't deserve to have fun.	That's my mother's belief. It is no longer mine.
I take care of myself and meet my needs.	How would he get along without me?	Probably just fine.
I take care of myself and meet my needs.	It's not right to be selfish.	I'm not being selfish when I love myself.

The affirmation-dialogue process helped Andrea to uncover her negative self-talk and replace it with positive and supportive statements. She also combined the sentences from the third column to create a powerful statement of what she wanted.

"I can take care of myself and meet my needs by asking for what I want. I am not being selfish when I love myself. I deserve to enjoy myself and have fun. John can learn to give to himself; he can do just fine when he is on his own."

Using Affirmations to Heal the Inner Child

As codependent people gradually become aware of and release their negative self-talk, other changes take place. Much of therapy is a process of reparenting. Affirmations can empower you to give yourself the positive messages that you needed, but never received, as a child. As you reparent the inner child through these loving and supportive words, that child will begin to love and appreciate itself as never before. This is how one client described her transformation:

Since I have begun to release my negative self-talk, I am experiencing myself as being in charge of my life instead of life being in charge of me. I now stand up for myself, whereas before I would have allowed others to walk over me. I love and appreciate myself more. In short, I am more in touch with who I am. I am living my own reality.

Health is a movement from environmental support to self-support, from listening to the "outer" voice to listening the "inner" voice. As you listen to your inner voice, you will become more aware of your own needs instead of denying them. Rather than unconsciously acting out the scripts of your parents and culture, the life you live will be your own.

This reality can become yours once you release the need to live through others and learn to follow your inner voice.

About the Author

   Douglas Bloch is an author, teacher, and counselor who writes on the subjects of psychology, healing, and spirituality. *Listening to Your Inner Voice* grew out of the quest to have his life directed by the Higher Power within. He is also the author of the inspirational books *Words That Heal: Affirmations and Meditations for Daily Living* and the forthcoming *I Am With You Always*.

   Douglas Bloch offers lectures and workshops on affirmations and other aspects of self-healing. You may contact him at 4226 NE Twenty-third Ave., Portland, OR 97211 (503) 284-2848.

WORDS TO LIVE BY meditation books
from CompCare Publishers

A Day at a Time
With nearly a million copies of the original edition in print, this recently reformatted version is slightly taller and wider and allows for larger type while maintaining a convenient pocket size. It includes a subject index. 03814, 365 pages, paperback

Twelve Months of Days
A pocket-sized book that has something for everyone seeking personal growth. Each daily entry includes a Twelve Step reflection, quotations, a "hunk of healing humor," and an affirmation. 03848, paperback, 370 pages

The Twelve Steps for Everyone
With nearly 300,000 copies in print since its original publication, this easy-to-understand book from grateful members of Emotional Health Anonymous, presents keys to emotional and spiritual health based on the Twelve Step of Alcoholics Anonymous. 03970, paperback, 365 pages

Order Form

Order No.	Qty.	Title	Author	Unit Cost	Total
04317		Listening to Your Inner Voice	Bloch, D. .	$8.95	
03814		A Day at a Time	Anonymous	$6.95	
03848		Twelve Months of Days	Rioux, D.	$6.95	
03970		The Twelve Steps for Everyone	Grateful Members	$6.95	
			Subtotal		
			Shipping and Handling (see below)		
			Add your state's sales tax		
			TOTAL		

Send check or money order payable to CompCare Publishers. No cash or C.O.D.'s please. Quantity discounts available. Prices subject to change without notice.

SHIPPING/HANDLING CHARGES

Amount of Order	Shipping Charges
$0.00-$10.00	$2.50
$10.01-$25.00	$3.50
$25.01-$50.00	$4.00
$50.01-$75.00	$5.00

Send book(s) to:

Name _____

Address _____

City _____ State _____ Zip _____

☐ Check enclosed for $_____, payable to CompCare Publishers

☐ Charge to my credit card ☐ Visa ☐ MasterCard ☐ Discover

Account # _____ Exp. date _____

Signature_____Daytime Phone _____

CompCare® Publishers

2415 Annapolis Lane, Minneapolis, MN 55441
To order by phone call toll free (800) 328-3330.
In Minnesota (612) 559-4800